Vitor Chaves de Oliveira

Unraveling IP Networks: Streaming

AF549448

Vitor Chaves de Oliveira

Unraveling IP Networks: Streaming

Find out how to measure Internet transmissions for quality in practice and which parameters affect each environment

ScienciaScripts

Imprint
Any brand names and product names mentioned in this book are subject to trademark, brand or patent protection and are trademarks or registered trademarks of their respective holders. The use of brand names, product names, common names, trade names, product descriptions etc. even without a particular marking in this work is in no way to be construed to mean that such names may be regarded as unrestricted in respect of trademark and brand protection legislation and could thus be used by anyone.

Cover image: www.ingimage.com

This book is a translation from the original published under ISBN 978-613-9-61418-9.

Publisher:
Sciencia Scripts
is a trademark of
Dodo Books Indian Ocean Ltd. and OmniScriptum S.R.L publishing group

120 High Road, East Finchley, London, N2 9ED, United Kingdom
Str. Armeneasca 28/1, office 1, Chisinau MD-2012, Republic of Moldova, Europe
Printed at: see last page
ISBN: 978-620-7-62839-1

Copyright © Vitor Chaves de Oliveira
Copyright © 2024 Dodo Books Indian Ocean Ltd. and OmniScriptum S.R.L publishing group

Table of contents:

I dedicate this work to my friend Alexandre de Assis Mota, who in his brief time showed me that everything we believe in is always worth fighting for. Someone who really "was heaven while he walked the earth" (Professor Doctor Antonio Meneghetti).
And I dedicate it to my parents.

ACKNOWLEDGMENTS

To Dr. Paulo Batista Lopes

My advisor, for his collaboration, his support and, of course, for the constant pressure that raises us to a greater understanding not only of research, but also of personal and professional training. I would like to thank him both for his exhaustive collaboration in the conception of this work and for his personal training.

To Dr. Gunnar Bedicks Junior

Director of EAD - Entidade Administradora da Digitali/acao da TV

To Dr. Alexandre de Assis Mota

Professor at PUC-Campinas.

To Dr. Lia Toledo Moreira Mota

Professor at PUC-Campinas.

To Dr. Edson Tafeli Carneiro dos Santos

Professor at Mackenzie Presbyterian University.

To Dr. Andreiwid Sheffer Correa

Professor at the Federal Institute of Education, Science and Technology of Sao Paulo - IFSP Campus Campinas

To. Dr. Paulo Alves Garcia

Professor at Mackenzie Presbyterian University

To Dr. Ismar Frango Silveira

Professor at Mackenzie Presbyterian University.

To Dr. Pollyana Notargiacomo Mustaro

Professor at Mackenzie Presbyterian University.

To Dr. Cristiano Akamine

Professor at Mackenzie Presbyterian University.

To Dr. Nizam Omar

Professor at Mackenzie Presbyterian University.

To Dr. Pedro Paulo Balbi

Professor at Mackenzie Presbyterian University.

To Dr. Marcelo Knorich Zuffo

Professor at the University of Sao Paulo.

To Dr. Yuzo laño

Professor at the State University of Campiñas

To my fellow Master's and PhD students for their collaborative support, especially Sérgio Bimbi Júnior, Waldemar Panadés Filho and Richard John Lintulahti Olandim for their encouragement and collaboration in the studies to complete this course.

To my colleagues and staff at the Digital TV Laboratory for their support.

To Secretary Yopanan Rocha for his collaboration in meeting requests.

To all the friends and colleagues from the various companies, research institutes and technical-scientific societies who supported me on this journey, especially SET - the Brazilian Television Engineering Society, SBC - the Brazilian Computer Society and IEEE - the Institute of Electrical and Electronics Engineers. And to everyone else I may not have mentioned.

UPM for encouraging research and extension by awarding scholarships to students, providing suitable laboratories and allocating qualified teaching staff to the Postgraduate Program in Electrical and Computer Engineering. As well as the infrastructure of a university that is competent and committed to its purpose. And that makes us proud to say the phrase, in which we honorably classify ourselves and are "Forever Mackenzistas!". At Mackenzie, the passion for science, for technology, for respect, for ethical and moral values guided by the principles of love for others is in the air we breathe. And we feel it all the time.

To God and, by association, to Christian principles, because no matter how much we study science and observe our lives, we know that He is there. And he convinced me day by day that he was always there. And he made me understand: "I will be with you and protect you wherever you go.", "Vanity of vanities... Everything is vanity!" and "Go on then, enjoy life with the one you love every day of your life and it will soon pass, just as mists and foams pass... Mist and foam... Everything is foam and foam".

"Always act in such a way that your behavior
can become the principle of a universal law."

Emmanuel Kant

SUMMARY

In the current IP video scenario, there is a lack of mechanisms to record two technical parameters that influence the commercial chain that sustains this entire Internet ecosystem: availability and audience. And the significant growth of this type of transmission continually rivals that of TV. With this in mind, and with the aim of measuring this new means of offering audiovisuals, this work has developed methodologies to acquire this information at the consumer end and to compare the viability of the transition from traditional broadcast TV to IP Streaming. This was done through a technical-mathematical comparison and the construction of two pieces of software, each with its own purpose, with their respective requirements analysis, as well as the method of how to interpret the results and infer how these parameters relate to each other. One was designed to measure the availability of any IP connection and is an application that can be used on various *browser* platforms. The other was implemented as an extension to one of the most widely used browsers, Google Chrome, to capture the Internet video audience on the largest video provider in existence today, Google's YouTube. In this work, the extraction of considerations around Quality of Service, QoS, is proposed to be interpreted as a measure of Quality of Experience, QoE, from the various total times and interactions of a video. To this end, given that the concept of quality translates into the particular subjectivity of each user and their individual expectations, the measurement of time is shown to be an effective evaluation. This effectiveness is justified by the principle of the consolidated audience measurement of TV broadcasting for decades. That is, the construction of something analogous to the 'People's meter' similar to the 'Television Rating Points', TRP, executing the capture of information that brings assertiveness to all stakeholders in this new delivery method. In this way, the user, the content producer, the advertiser, the platform owner, the owner of the content delivery network (CDN) and the internet service provider (ISP) can all be measured with the same level of reliability.
Index Terms: IP Stream, TV Broadcast, Audience, Connection Availability, Quality of Service (QoS), Quality of Experience (QoE), Software Development.

Chapter 1

1. INTRODUCTION

This chapter discusses the problematization of the research, as well as the motivations and division of the thesis.

1.1. Background to the problem

In the current context of broadcasting audiovisual content, the so-called new media have gained considerable ground, to the point where they are routinely rivaled by traditional television broadcasting, or Broadcast TV. Certain statistical analyses show that traditional television broadcasting via radio, cable and satellite technology is steadily losing ground to media content delivered via the Internet. As a result, a scenario is emerging in which more and more content is offered on demand to the user. As a result, consumers expect to receive audio and video whenever and wherever they want (Edwards, 2013; Ellacott, 2014; Frost, 2014). However, the quality benchmark for the delivery of this data that makes up the audiovisual stream has been established by the TV and this is the user's expectation (Oliveira *et al*, 2015 A; McMillan, 2013). In other words, a network based on the packet-switched Internet Protocol (IP) is expected to behave, in terms of communication quality, like a circuit-switched network (Katel, 2014; Octoshape & T-Mobile, 2014; Chaves de Oliveira *et al,* 2016 A, Chaves de Oliveira et *al, 2016*, Kaduoka et al, 2016 , Oliveira *et al,* 2015 B). Thus, there is a growing need to compare and guarantee the assertiveness established and consolidated in Broadcast TV for video streaming via IP, or IP Stream (Oliveira *et al*, 2015 B).

In this sense, it is necessary to point out that this new system of communication does not offer any guarantee of quality by default, being a service categorized as 'best effort', or *Best-Effort* (Tanenbaum & Wetherall, 2010). This means that there is no standard for delivering a certain amount of bits per time interval. In other words, the video stream is variable depending on traffic and competition for the channel is not controlled, since the IP protocol stack, designed to interconnect telecommunications systems in a simple and effective way, only controls the higher layers. And the layer that dictates this operation is the highest, which deals directly with the interface exposed to the user, the application layer (Tanenbaum & Wetherall, 2010; Ross and Kurose, 2013), at the level of location of the physical end of the network and the logical end of the software, both in the consumer. In other words, on the user's machine and at the level of this application layer, where the consumer takes a leading role in choosing the video content that is delivered to them (Tanenbaum & Wetherall, 2010; Ross and Kurose, 2013). Consequently, the whole perception of quality lies at this end and monitoring it becomes more important in order to protect the stakeholders involved in the commercial chain of this new ecosystem.

1.2. Justification for developing the work

Given the growth of the video-on-demand model, the search for mechanisms that bring security to the commercial chain that supports it is becoming a growing necessity. Ensuring quality in a service that is not connection-oriented like traditional TV requires constant and continuous monitoring and evaluation. This metrication of transmission must take place at the user's end, both for technical reasons and for reasons of moral hazard, in order to prevent one entity from being in charge of monitoring itself.

Considering these issues, we need to analyze the entire business chain involved in the so-called Broadband Stream, i.e. IP Stream via broadband, relating the technological part to the commercial part. In other words, list all the participants who are risking their interests in terms of the availability and quality of the stream. As an example, and this is one of the focuses of this work because it is the largest provider of video on demand, we could evaluate the commercial operation of YouTube today. It manages to get entire industries to maintain and release content continuously on its platform, whether they are music artists with clips, record labels, comedians, teachers, vloggers (independent producers), TV networks, etc. And it pays those who post these videos by number of views. In this way, it holds the supply of content on its site instead of these content producers seeking out competitors such as Vimeo or Dailymotion. The funds that finance this business model come from advertisements placed before and during the video or on the side of the screen. These ads are paid for by counting the number of views, or clicks. It's worth remembering that ad marketing is done through artificial intelligence statistical relationships with data obtained over time, by user profile. (Statista, 2015 A; Statista, 2016)

With this in mind and knowing that the platform provider does not have stream control over what and how users receive or don't receive the content they demand, vulnerabilities are highlighted. These are risks that affect the management of the business and commercial transactions require guarantees that must go beyond the limitations of the IP system. In other words, providing a certain level of security for the content producer, the advertiser and the user is important. Data on the quality and availability of content dictates whether these services meet or fall short of what is required, or whether they harm business interests. Therefore, it is imperative to note that, objectively, the only consolidated information that can be offered from the IP Stream is the click count, since additional information could only be observed at the end by Content Delivery Network (CDN) providers, for example: Akamai, Edge, etc.by Internet Service Providers (ISPs), for example: Comcast, AT&T, Time Warner Cable and by the owners of the web platforms on which the content is accessed by users, for example: Youtube, Vimeo, Dailymotion.

At this point an important point emerges, that of moral hazard, observed by the dynamics of each entity connected technically and directly with the delivery being obliged to supervise itself. Suppose the following situations exist:

- a problem with transmission in which the CDN is responsible for the small number of servers in the last mile or for excessive access consuming bandwidth that is less than necessary;
- the ISP has a problem of not having enough available flow to serve the content provider or serve the CDN to sustain the connection on a certain branch of its network because it has sold more than there is physical bandwidth (overbooking) or because of a technical difficulty of broken equipment or a broken cable or channel;
- the content provider has a software failure to send ads to the CDN;
- the platform holder incurs software errors making it impossible to view;

In all of these situations, an entity should inform its client that it has partial or total problems and face penalties. Therefore, your motivation to invest in self-monitoring always comes up against something potentially harmful to your business.

As a result, there is a notable risk involved for the IP Stream industry that hardly exists for Broadcast TV. This is because in traditional TV it is difficult for a problem to go unnoticed, both for technical reasons such as measuring the signal-to-noise ratio (SNR) or power (dBm, decibel milliwatt) of the received signal and for commercial reasons related to the audience. This is explained: the television audience is measured by sampling with devices installed in users' televisions and this provides subsidies for a TV channel in composing its price for advertisements. Furthermore, in TV broadcasting, a transmission problem usually affects many users or often all of them. Therefore, the advertiser can easily know if his ad has been successfully delivered without depending on his contractor to inform him. For the web stream, this is uncertain, since a user who is next to a CDN server may receive an adequate service and his neighbor in the same city, but far from a CDN server or with a server that is too busy, may have the same content unavailable to him. In other words, the ISP, the content provider, the CDN and the platform owner end up publicizing or even knowing that they are 'down' only when the problem is of considerable proportions. However, the ephemeral problems inherent in IP technology are not clearly publicized. And since they don't measure what is being delivered, they are shielded by this. This is because in order to know what is happening at the user's end, they would have to have a device similar to a TV audience monitor. Remember that the current audience paid for by the advertiser is based on paying per click, or view, without knowing if it has actually been delivered and/or to satisfaction.

In addition, in this work, in order to interpret the results of the software that verifies the audience and availability, Quality of Service (QoS) was considered as a concept of Quality of Experience (QoE), i.e. based on the time watched compared to the total duration of a video. This is because, given that the concept of quality translates into the particular subjectivity of each user and their individual expectations, the measurement of time proves to be an effective evaluation, since the user only continues to watch content that is in line with what they expect in technical terms and in line with what they want in terms of production. This interpretation is verified as correct through the principle of the consolidated measurement of TV broadcast audience for decades by the People's meter in the Television Rating Points (TRP) scheme.

1.3. Objective of the work

In this work, the general objective was to develop ways of evaluating and possibly analogously bringing parts of the assertiveness, i.e. the certainty and confidence, of Broadcast TV to IP Stream, in order to measure the quality of audiovisual content delivery, in terms of costs, availability and audience.

To this end, three specific objectives were considered:

1- Evaluate the cost and technical feasibility of replacing this new service in terms of cost in terms of throughput and the purpose of broadcasting live or not;

2- Assess the availability of IP connections in a segregated manner; and

3- Capture the audience associated with the availability of the IP video stream

4- Analyze the captured data.

In this sense, software-based methodologies were built to measure the delivery of audiovisual content at the physical and logical end of the user, i.e. programs that act on the user's machine and at the application layer level. The data captured was also analyzed in order to understand the role of availability and audience.

1.4. Research delimitation

This work is delimited as follows to build the solution to each of the aforementioned specific objectives:

1 - A technical-mathematical comparison was made of IP Stream throughput versus TV Broadcast throughput for the communication channel. The existing consumption of recent digital TV systems currently in use was considered, citing ISDB-T, ATSC, DVB-T and DMB-T as examples. And for IP networks, it was calculated for IPv4, IPv6 and hybrid networks that combine both standards. This evaluation is complemented by technical solution design considerations via CDNs and ISPs;

2 - A software program was built with a web interface, based on the Java language and a database in the SQL language, to check the availability of any resources on an IP network, such as videos. This program has been consolidated as an application that can be used on various web browser platforms;

3 - Software was built with a web interface, based on JavaScript and a database in SQL language, configured exclusively as an extension for one of the most widely used browsers, Google Chrome (Statista, 2015 B), programmed to capture the audience and availability of videos offered on the Internet by the largest video provider in existence today, Google's YouTube (Statista, 2015A; Statista, 2016).

4 - The data was analyzed so that the experiment can be reproduced even when the information in the YouTube API changes, as it did during the course of this work. In other words, so that the software that captures the information can always be built or remodeled, since the Google platform can modify the desired parameters. In this way, we define which parameters are necessary and which analysis should be carried out with the data in order to gauge availability and audience. This software is limited to operating only on devices that support this browser, with the possibility of enabling extensions. It's worth noting that due to the size of the universe YouTube itself is part of, of the order of 2 quadrillion views a year (Statistic Brain, 2016; Youtube, 2017), statistical analyses with a sufficient number of samples and users, given that the order of these is 1.3 billion were not numerous enough to evaluate YouTube, as explained in section 5.3.2.3 of this paper. In addition, the platform is limited, since more than half of the videos accessed on YouTube are via *smartphones* (Statistic Brain, 2016; Youtube, 2017). However, the precepts and the creation of mechanisms to capture and evaluate availability and audience in order to demonstrate what is relevant in this measurement can be applied to the entire world of IP content. In addition, in order to partially outline the mobile part, and since the objective is to measure connections, part of the tests

were carried out using mobile networks through a cell phone routing its internet connection to a notebook.

1.5. Text organization

This work is divided as follows.

Chapter 1, Introduction: contextualizes the topic, presents the justification for its study, describes the objective of the work and delimits the actions present in this research.

Chapter 2, Audiovisual Content Transmission: describes how TV Broadcast and IP Stream work, covering: the IP architecture, content delivery networks (CDNs) and internet service providers (ISPs).

Chapter 3, Quality of Video Transmission: discusses the definition of Quality of Service parameters, QoS, relating it to the issue of resource availability in IP networks. It also describes Quality of Experience, QoE, from the perspective of user perception through audience metrics.

Chapter 4, Methodology: shows how the following were conceived and built: the Technical-Mathematical Comparative IP Stream vs. TV Broadcast, the Software for Gauging Connection Availability and the Software for Video Stream Audience Capture, describing all the stages of each process. Including, for the computer programs, requirements analysis and detailed development. The requirements analysis part stands out because it contains the parameters defined to be captured, as they are fundamental for analyzing the subject.

Chapter 5, Results: presents a Technical-Mathematical Comparison of IP Stream vs. TV Broadcast: the cost in terms of throughput and the cost in terms of the technical solution of replacing one with the other; presents the Software for Gauging Connection Availability, how it works and the data captured; presents the Software for Capturing Video Stream Audience, how it works and the data captured, as well as an analysis of how to interpret this data.

Chapter 6, Conclusion: provides a discussion of the results obtained and the aforementioned implementations, considers the impacts imposed on the subject and outlines possible developments for future work.

Chapter 7, Suggestions for Possible Future Work: points out further work that could be carried out on the basis of this thesis.

Chapter 8, References: lists all the bibliographical references presented in this work.

Chapter 2

2. TRANSMISSION OF AUDIOVISUAL CONTENT

This stage of the text explores the issue of transmitting audiovisual content electronically, i.e. digitally, by the main means used today.

2.1. TV Broadcast

The aim of this introductory session is to explain the state of the art in traditional TV broadcasting, which is specifically governed by digital modulation techniques.

The digitization of TV signals is a worldwide trend, both because of the demand for content with higher sound and image quality and because of the scarcity of spectrum (Bedicks, 2008). There are four main digital terrestrial transmission standards that make up the current technology landscape (Bedicks, 2008). These include the North American standard ATSC, or *Advanced Television Systems Committee,* which uses 8-VSB modulation, or *Eight-Vestigial Side Band.* the European standard DVB-T, or *Digital Video Broadcasting - Terrestrial*, which uses COFDM modulation, or *Coded Orthogonal Frequency Division Multiplex*, the Chinese standard DMB-T, or *Digital Multimedia Broadcast-Terrestrial*, which uses TDS-OFDM modulation, or *Time Domain Synchronization - Orthogonal Frequency Division Multiplexing,* and the standard used in Japan and Brazil with minor variations, ISDB-T, or *Integrated Services Digital Broadcasting Terrestrial*, which uses BST-OFDM modulation, or *Band-Segmented Transmission Orthogonal Frequency Division Multiplexing*. Considering high definition transmissions, a video called Full HD (*High Definition*), or 1K, associated with the audio stream, for a large 16:9 screen and images up to 1920*1080 pixels in size, requires a throughput of around 19.3 Mbits per second on most of these digital TV standards in use today (Oliveira *et al*, 2015 B).

2.2. IP Stream

In order to contribute to the theme of audiovisual content transmission, this part contextualizes the flow of information by packets, led by the so-called Internet Protocol (IP).

2.2.1. IP architecture

Since IP architecture is the one that is becoming increasingly present in real terms, the focus of this section is to explain this subject.

Streaming media via the Internet protocol has become a common means of content delivery today (Edwards, 2013; Frost, 2014; McMillan, 2013). And it is literally slowly taking over the role of traditional TV as the main content broadcaster (Edwards, 2013; Frost, 2014; McMillan, 2013). However, the latest live broadcasts have shown that this migration still has a long way to go (Chai, 2014; Greenfield, 2012; Sharma and FitzGerald, 2014). The reason for this is that although the technology already exists, the bandwidth is often not available. Initially, it is necessary to clarify that the flow requirement is dictated by the same technology that makes it possible for this on-demand content model to exist (Tanenbaum & Wetherall, 2010; Ross and Kurose, 2013). Furthermore, the Internet Protocol (IP) is, in a way, a victim of its own success, since, due to its ubiquity in this digital century, newer versions are needed to reflect the evolution of the network itself. For example, with the evolution from IP version 4 (IPv4) to version 6 (IPv6) of computer communications, new obstacles have arisen since hybrid networks will always be present, and these use both standards, swapping from one to the other, increasing the cost of throughput with bottlenecks (Tanenbaum & Wetherall, 2010; Ross and Kurose, 2013). Alongside this, today's average user expects a considerable High Definition (HD) experience (Oliveira *et al*, 2015 A; Oliveira *et al, 2015* B). All these technical costs involved in delivering IP video are naturally transformed into monetary values at some point. At this point, it's interesting to remember that, given the global trend for telecommunications to be treated as a commoditized good, large infrastructure investments are avoided (Kenyon and Cheliotis, 2001; Hughes, 2010; Oliveira *et al,* 2015 A, Kaduoka *et al,* 2016). Therefore, companies today are challenged with the mission of designing solutions that are as affordable as possible. This means making the most of the bandwidth available to them on cable and free-to-air channels. As well as acting to avoid channel clogging in this stochastic global packet network, i.e. the web.

In order to manage throughput to ensure channel availability, especially for large IP video

streams, a mathematical evaluation of throughput costs gains importance.
Through this analysis, it is possible to know how to limit the number of users of a given live event and how much bandwidth needs to be acquired for its operation, depending on the number of clients. In addition, it can also indicate whether it is interesting to deliver this content via traditional TV broadcasting, since most end-user devices nowadays are prepared for this (Doeven, 2013). And, given the high standards of quality and availability present in TV broadcasts for decades (Bedicks, 2008), this option should be considered. In addition, the discussion of hybrid solutions should be budgeted for, as this can allow for geographical and technological segmentation, and achieve the desired objectives.

This paper discusses useful data and methods for comparing IPTV and traditional TV in order to help plan and design solutions for the delivery of live and recorded video. In the following sections, content transfer strategies are presented, followed by calculation bases for evaluations.

2.2.2. Content Delivery Network (CDN) and Internet Service Provider (ISP)

A *Content* Delivery *Network* (CDN) is an implementation of techniques designed to improve efficiency in the delivery and distribution of media content to end users over the Internet (Rouse, 2011; Octoshape & T-Mobile, 2014). As a broadband provider (BP), the *Internet Service Provider* (ISP), or Internet Access Provider, is usually a telecommunications company that sells bandwidth, measured in Mbps (Megabits per second), which connects customers to the World Wide Web, i.e. the Internet (ITU, 2003; Christensson, 2014). From these descriptions we can see the close relationship of dependency shared by CDNs, ISPs and the issue of content availability.

CDN techniques translate into a hardware and software arrangement that defines numerous servers dispersed in locations that automatically replicate content based on user preferences acquired through artificial intelligence algorithms (Buyya *et al*, 2008). The initial idea is to physically place computers that will form a shorter communication route, in terms of the number of nodes, with consumers. In a second step, the proposal for these computers is storage, i.e. keeping a copy of the content that users can, or are more likely to, access and/or request. Thus, the web path is reduced, increasing network availability, because there are fewer devices that make up *FullNetworkAvailability* (FNA). The evaluation for this gain is the fact that, with more sources to provide the service, it can be considered that there are more clusters, or replicators, agglomerated with others, so the whole system becomes more reliable. The schematic presenting the CDN mechanism is shown below in Figure 1. It shows how the data is transmitted from the origin servers, then to the caching servers also called last mile servers and finally, closer to their end users. These end users are exemplified by different devices: tablets, laptops, desktops and cell phones. Completing this illustration is the role of the Internet Service Provider (ISP) who provides these connections.

Figure 1: Schematic of a Content Delivery Network (CDN) showing the flow of data through Internet Service Provider (ISP) connections.

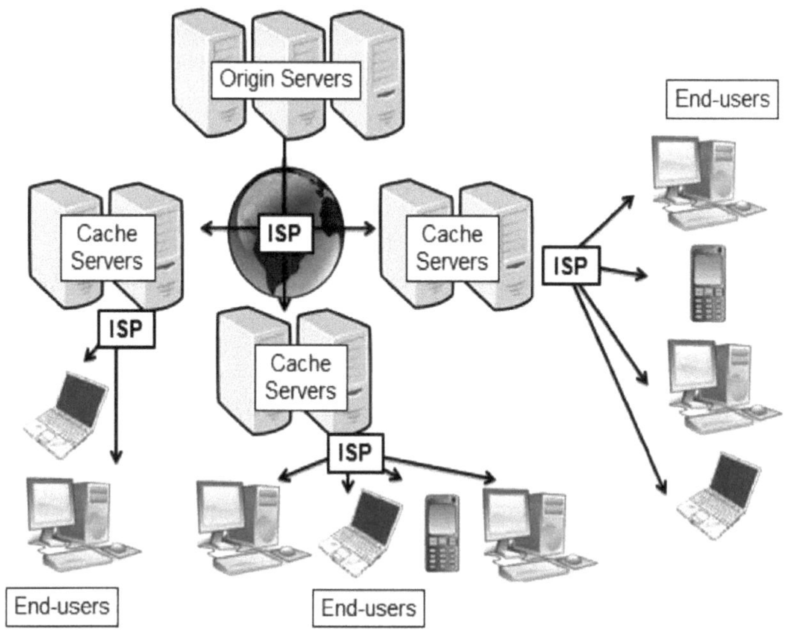

Source: Adapted and Reproduced from METHODOLOGY TO ASSES IP CONNECTION... (OLIVEIRA *et al* ,2015 A)

From this CDN strategy, two main characteristics are drawn: the focus on improving access to content and the dependence on Broadband Providers (ISPs) at various levels of the system. The latter fundamentally circles back to concerns about availability. Hence understanding the role of the ISP or BP is imperative.

A broadband provider regularly has a predetermined obligation to ensure that a certain amount of bandwidth is offered to the customer at all times. In the same way, it is implicit that, for a connection service to have any kind of contractually defined bit-per-second throughput compliance, it must respond accordingly; that is, it must be available. However, an erroneous contractual justification can be assumed by disregarding the availability issue even when displaying true information. Consider, for example, that the average throughput during a video transmission lasting 100 minutes was 2.5 Mbps and that there is a contractual agreement with an ISP that indicates a minimum bandwidth of 2.0 Mbps. Some might claim that the service was compliant. But now consider that the connection was disconnected for 50 minutes, i.e. transmitting at 0.0 Mbps rate, and that for the other 50 minutes it ran at a constant rate of 5.0 Mbps. At this point, the problem of analysis based solely on transfer rate arises. Since, in the forged example, the client can't see half of the video, a service rating of unsatisfactory is clear, and goes completely against the previous analysis. The graph plotted below in Figure 2 elucidates this situation, expressing how an average is inefficient data to take into account. This calculation of average *throughput* is presented in Equation 1 (Oliveira *et al*, 2015 A) below the graph. From the graph it is possible to visualize the calculated average, for all the time it refers to, in relation to the 'real' measured flow. The calculated average graph line implies a good connection service for the entire hundred minutes, disregarding the fact that, in reality, the flow only occurred for the first fifty minutes and it was switched off for the second half.

In addition, it is vital to remember that a CDN as well as the ISP share objective responsibility for providing content to end users. Both need to be accessible in order for the network to operate successfully. And the most important operation in content delivery on IP networks today is video streaming (TECHNAVIO, 2014).

Figure 2: Throughput network connection assessment in an IP Video Stream transmission. **Source:** Adapted and Reproduced from METHODOLOGY TO ASSES IP CONNECTION... (OLIVEIRA *et al*,2015 A)

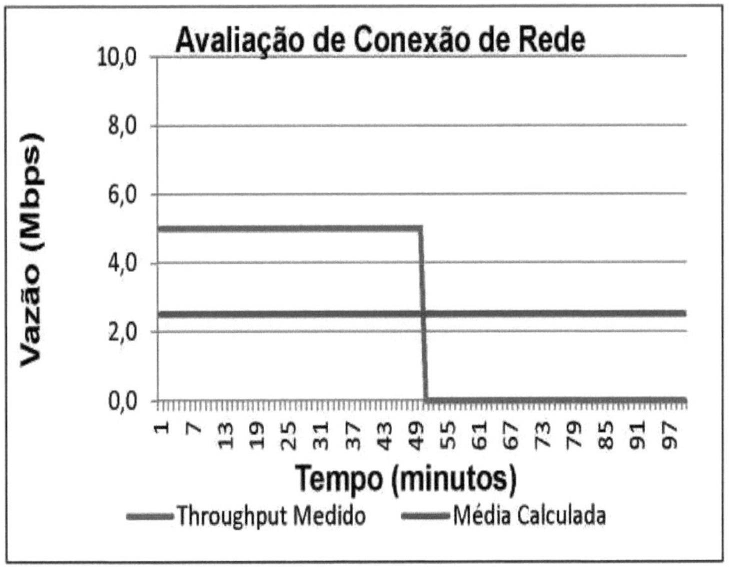

$$\text{Throughput Médio (Mbps)} = \frac{\text{bits transferidos (Megabits)}}{\text{Tempo (segundos)}} \quad (1)$$

Chapter 3

3. VIDEO TRANSMISSION QUALITY

Video quality in packet networks, i.e. IP networks, has been a constant concern in order to obtain a satisfactory content stream. This chapter aims to discuss these concepts.

3.1. Quality of Service QoS

In computer networks, i.e. Internet protocol networks, Quality of Service is a set of technical conditions that permeate a qualitative operation for a given application that relies on an IP network to function (Oliveira *et al*, 2013 A; Baldini *et al,* 2014). These requirements translate into specific QoS parameters in computer networks, such as throughput, latency, *jitter* and losses (Oliveira *et al*, 2013 B;; Khanafer et al, 2014). The first parameter, known as throughput, refers to the amount of data transmitted per time interval, measured in bits per second (bps) or bytes per second (Bps). Latency, or delay, indicates the time taken for packets to be transmitted from the point of origin (or node) to the point of destination (or node). While *jitter* corresponds to the delay variation time, i.e. the difference in time taken by data packets to travel from the transmitter to the receiver. As for losses, these correspond to data detriments that occur in transmission that damage the information of bit segments. Losses can be represented by the bit error rate, or BER (*Bit Error Rate*), the packet error rate, or PER (*Packet Error Rate)*, or frame error rates, or FER (*Frame Error Rate*), all of which are usually measured in percentages (%). (Oliveira, 2012; Nunes, 2011)

3.1.1. Availability

All these parameters are related to the concept of availability. Essentially, it precedes it, so that for any of these parameters to be measured, the connection must first be available (Doeven, 2013). Therefore, it is established that the concept of availability is classified as the first concern with quality, even for basic service standards. As such, it becomes prominent to define and quantify this. And, a mathematical calculation of probabilities is how this statistic is estimated and only through real experimental measurements can it be provided. Initially, to understand that, in order to estimate availability, it is necessary to know that all the devices present on the network individually have a probability of failure. This failure depends on two main factors that form what is usually called expected downtime: equipment failure and *failover*, which is the time taken for technical repairs. The former is usually listed in the *data sheet* for each piece of equipment and the latter is provided by the company that supports the operation with technical personnel. In this way, availability is considered to be the probability, in the event of an estimate, that a service, or a device, will be available for a period of time. Therefore, subtracting from 1 (100%) the sum of the *Average Expected Downtime of the Device* (AEDD) and the Average *Time* to Repair the Device (ATRD) divided by the *Total Period of Time (*TPT). Equation 2 (Oliveira *et al*, 2015 A) describes the mathematical calculation used to describe the availability of a *Single NetworkEquipment (*ASNE) given as a percentage (N-TRON, 2014; (Oliveira *et al,* 2015 A).

$$\text{ASNE (\%)} = 1 - \frac{\text{AEDD} + \text{ATRD}}{\text{TPT}} (\text{x}100) \qquad (2)$$

With this in mind, it becomes possible to consider the complete availability of the network. This is achieved by first calculating the availability of each device and multiplying it by the entire network, from end to end. In other words, multiplying the individual availability of the first network equipment, or *Availability of a Single Network Equipment* 1 (ASNE-1: First Device) by the availability of Equipment 2 (ASNE-2) and so on (up to the last device), thus giving the complete availability of the network, or *Full Network Availability (*FNA). This equation is shown as follows in Equation 3, which is always made up of devices, knowing which is an impractical task for networks such as the Internet. (N-TRON, 2014; Oliveira *et al*, 2015 A)

$$\text{FNA(\%)} = \text{ASNE-1} * \text{ASNE-2} * \ldots * \text{ASNE-Last Device } (\text{x}100) \qquad (3)$$

Exploring these statistical estimation calculations, it is implied that the communication path needs to be fully known in order to apply them. This means that it is necessary to know the ASNE of each server, switch, router, repeater, cable line, etc. between the source and destination in order to calculate it. But, on closer examination of this subject, it is possible to imagine the difficulty of carrying out this calculation, because the connection is via the Internet and the equipment that is connected to the connection route can vary stochastically. In addition, it should be remembered that web connections are formed dynamically for each packet of data that is channeled, generally using Dijkstra's shortest path algorithm and/or some derivations of it (Dijkstra, 1959). Thus, availability estimation cannot be carried out, because the TCP / IP (*Transmission Control Protocol / Internet Protocol)* model, on which computer networks are based, does not normally transmit any detailed information about what type of equipment (brand, type, etc.) is routed through them and implementing an information transmission solution would be unfeasible due to the expensive increase in *overhead*, in addition to useful data, in the transfer rate (Ross and Kurose, 2013).

Following this logic, it is recognized that a method for evaluating the availability of an Internet connection service requires, by definition, an experimental approach. And only then, through mathematical modeling of the data previously collected, can statistical metrics be generated to define expectations for service availability. However, it is imperative to assume that such an estimate would only be valid for each physical connection of each end user. An experimental arrangement proposed for constructing such an estimate is achieved by uninterrupted collection and archiving of information obtained through network monitoring. Along with this, a calculation is equally crucial to produce the intended availability metric. This *Experimentally Measured Full Network Availability (*EMFNA) is indicated by subtracting from 1 (100%) the sum of the time duration referring to all measured failures, or '*All the Measured Failure Times' (*AMFT) divided by the total period of time, or *Total Period of Time (*TPT), shown as follows in Equation 4. (N-TRON, 2014; Oliveira *et al,* 2015 A)

$$\text{EMFNA}(\%) = 1 - \frac{\text{AMFT}}{\text{TPT}} (\times 100) \quad (4)$$

Another relevant aspect in an experimental set-up to observe whether a connection is available refers to the fact that the data collected must be time-stamped. This additional information would help to detect certain periods of the day, week, month or year when the network service is more or less likely to be working properly, reinforcing the importance of time-stamping, especially for live CDN transmissions, since these could be scheduled during better periods of availability. Or, at least, the customer could know the likelihood of their call being available at the scheduled times in advance. In addition, the customer would also be able to discern the best periods, in terms of connection, to watch their on-demand video from the CDNs' IP streams.

3.2. Quality of Experience QoE

When we look at the definition of Quality of Experience as dictated by the *International* Telecommunication *Union* (ITU), we see the following:

"The general acceptability of an application or service, as subjectively perceived by the end user.

NOTE 1 - Quality of Experience includes the complete end-to-end effects of the system (customer, terminal, network, infrastructure services, etc.).

NOTE 2 - general acceptability can be influenced by user expectations and context."

Taken entirely from *Definition of Quality of Experience (QoE)* (ITU, 2007).

The aforementioned QoS parameters, flow, latency, jitter, losses and availability, transform the effects of the sensitivity and perception of a video transmission, affecting what is evaluated as the Quality of Experience that the end user perceives and receives. Figure 3 below shows, in the form of an objective flowchart, how this is related. It shows how Quality of Experience is affected by the aforementioned Quality of Service parameters. Furthermore, in this image it is possible to detect the feedback between QoE and QoS, considering the user's perception and evaluation expectations as part of the qualitative definition process (TELECO, 2008; NORTEL *et al* 2006). However, it should be noted that although QoE is closely linked to Qos, it is not exclusively understood by Quality of Service, since it is subjective, i.e. there are variations from one end user to another (ITU, 2007).

Figure 3: Interdependence between QoS and QoE.

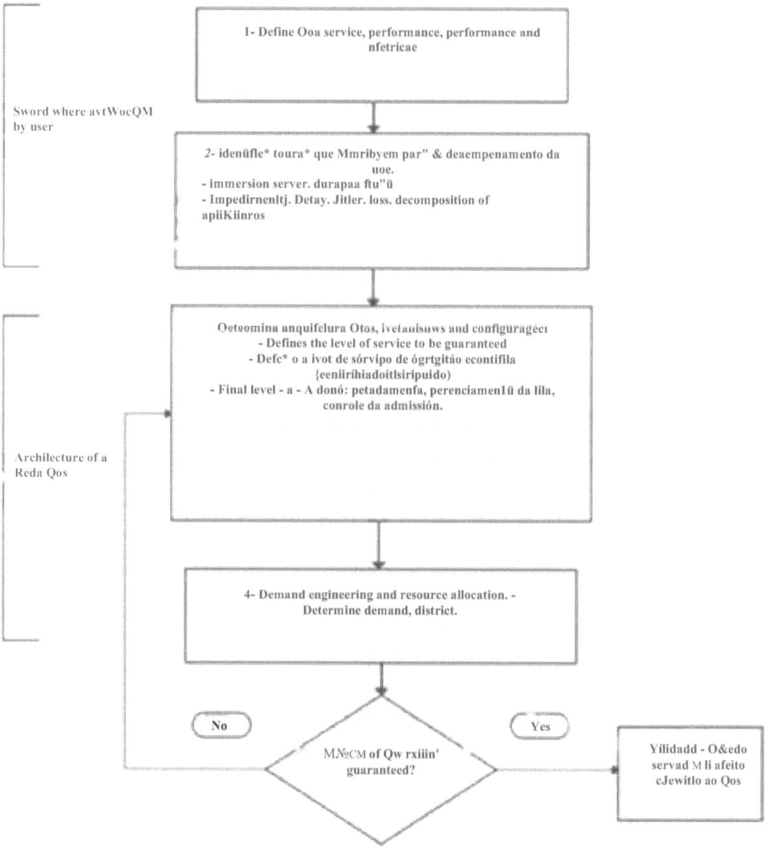

Source: Reproduced from SEQÁO TUTORIAIS BANDA LARGA (TELECO, 2008) | Figure adapted (NORTEL *et al*, 2006).

In addition, it is worth noting that the standard for subjectively analyzing QoE in relation to video quality recommends a comparison of five image classifications as a reference, graded at different quality levels, as shown in Figure 4.

In order to understand the image represented by Figure 4, it is necessary to recall the concepts of Information Theory (Shannon, 1948) which have been extended to analyze the concept of Entropy. Therefore, in order to understand the objectivity we want with image and frame analysis, it is necessary to relate the bits or bytes per second to the variation in the amount of information trafficked, represented by entropy. That is, the higher the entropy, the greater the information and consequently the greater the flow (bits and bytes). And the higher the entropy, the better the picture will be visualized and perceived by the user. This assessment is certainly correct, but it is incomplete when error rates are taken into account. These harmful effects deteriorate the information transmitted and the quality perceived by the user. And, for traditional TV, there are defined parameters for the relationship between correct and incorrect bits so that we can correct this problem by technical means. However, for IP networks the analysis is not so simple, because the greater the number of errors, the greater the entropy, due to retransmissions by the very nature of the technology. Or even greater deterioration of the image to adapt to the available throughput through computational techniques that reduce the frame, and consequently its quality. In short, the image in Figure 4 serves as a guide for measuring these effects in any type of audiovisual content transmission.

In addition, it is worth noting that in this context the issue of availability is consistently highlighted, since it shows that the quality of the audiovisual content signal is representative of audience engagement. And if this deteriorates, the loss of views follows this trend consistently. This is evidenced by data and mathematical correlations (Krishnan & Sitaraman, 2013) and for copyright reasons and because it uses corporate information, this information and graphics cannot be reproduced in this thesis.

Figure 4: Subjective image quality ITU-5 BT.500-13.

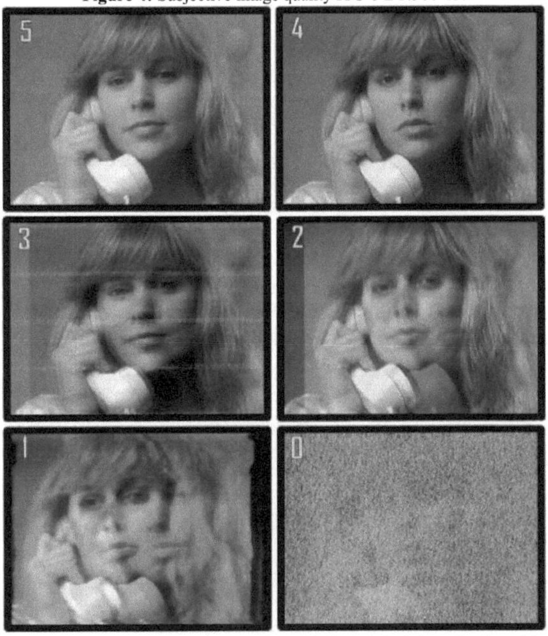

Source: Reproduced from RECOMMENDATION ITU-R BT.500-13 - Methodology for the subjective assessment of the quality of television pictures | Figure adapted (ITU, 2012).

The categorization scale of five evaluates the degrees of fault in an image as follows, according to ITU-R BT.500-13:

a) 5 Imperceptible - When it is at the maximum level of quality expected by the user, when 100% of expectations are met.
b) 4 Perceptible, but not bothersome - When the quality is not ideal, but the flaws do not cause so much discomfort despite the expectation not being 100% met.
c) 3 Somewhat annoying - When the quality is considered reasonable, it is still possible to see the image with a certain level of clarity, even with questionable satisfaction.
d) 2 Irritating - When the flaws leave the image with poor or bad quality, causing discomfort with the whole picture being viewed, although it is possible to understand the image, even if unsatisfactorily.
e) 1 Very annoying - When the flaws affect the entire image and the discomfort for the user is complete and for the entire picture viewed, being evaluated as very poor quality, the image may not be understood in part or in its entirety.
f) 0 No signal - When there are no signals distinguishable enough to even know that a transmission is taking place.

It's worth pointing out, through this ITU concept, that QoE refers to user expectations and that there are no defined values for these levels, which is subjective and requires a joint effort with user groups to quantify these levels. However, this concept is not used for the purposes of this work, as the focus is on studying the cost in terms of throughput, availability and audience of audiovisual content on IP networks.

1 .2.1 Hearing

The concepts listed so far in this article are closely related to the definition of audience for audiovisual content, described below.

"Meaning of Audience

5 .f. A gathering of individuals (listeners or viewers) who, by assumption, survey, estimate or statistical evidence, watch certain television or radio programs."

Taken entirely from Meaning of Audience (DICIO, 2016).

In order to practically measure the audience for content broadcast on Broadcast TV, a piece of equipment called a people meter or audience meter is used. This is installed in the homes of certain viewers and connected to their television sets, recording and sending information to a central station on a continuous basis about which channel is being watched, at what time and for how long. These users are chosen to have these devices installed in their homes so that all of them represent a portrait, a sample, of the whole of society or the segment of society that you want to measure. All this equipment is called Television *Rating* Points (TRP), which aggregates the entire measurement system. In this way, the amount of success of audiovisual content is statistically estimated. Audience measurement is important because it drives the commercial side of which programs a broadcaster should or shouldn't invest in and the impact or reach of advertising campaigns. There is thus a relevant commercial interest for the purposes of pricing broadcasting periods in this and other segments such as IP Streaming. (IBOPE, 2015; ATO, 2015; GFK, 2015).

Chapter 4

4. METHODOLOGY

The method used in this research is detailed in this chapter with the three main works aimed at achieving the desired objectives, with a great deal of attention paid to the construction of control mechanisms for video on demand in the IP ecosystem. In addition, it should be noted that this research is supported and based on the so-called DSR, or *Design Science Research* and *The Sciences of the artificial,* which deal with the construction of artifacts to solve real-world problems, thus representing that software, models, algorithms, methods, analysis, information systems and entities form a scientific method (Dresch *et al*, 2015; Simon, 1996).

4.1. Technical-Mathematical Comparison IP Stream versus TV Broadcast

The cost of IP architecture and digital Broadcast TV is described below for the purposes of comparing channel costs, in terms of throughput for each type of implementation.

4.1.1. IP Stream

The strategy of encapsulating networks for video transmission has gained ground in recent decades by allowing links to be shared and thus maximizing the accessibility of telecommunications in general, transforming circuit switching into a non-competitive adoption in relation to the diffusion of videos via stream. Thus, understanding the mathematical theory embedded in packet networks in terms of the accumulation or increase of bits to encapsulate data becomes relevant in the quest to escape events that bring down the network, called *cord-cutters* (Chai, 2014; Greenfield, 2012; Sharma and FitzGerald, 2014). Specifically, it is crucial to focus on analyzing IPv4 (Internet Protocol version 4) and IPv6 (Internet Protocol version 6), which together make up the main communication networks today (Babatunde and Al-Debagy, 2014).

The Internet Protocol version 4 has the following header format, summarized in Figure 5.

Figure 5: Schematic of the Internet Protocol version 4 header.

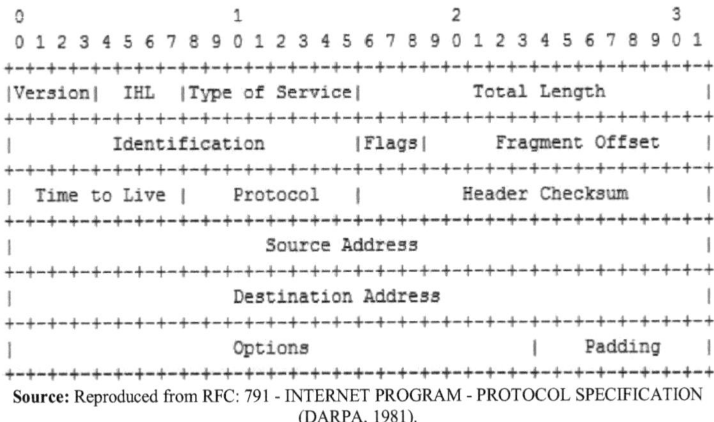

Source: Reproduced from RFC: 791 - INTERNET PROGRAM - PROTOCOL SPECIFICATION (DARPA, 1981).

Figure 5 exemplifies the typical internet header in IPv4, requiring 20 octets or 20 bytes, i.e. 160 bits of information are added via data segments to form datagrams which are usually fixed at 576 bytes. This initially increases costs by 3.4722% over the total *throughput. It is* also worth mentioning that the header can be as long as 60 octets and the datagram packet is capable of reaching up to 65,535 bytes, but these sizes are not yet the criteria used. (DARPA, 1981; Oliveira *et al*,2015 B)

Internet Protocol version 6 has the following header format, summarized in Figure 6.

Figure 6: Schematic of the Internet Protocol version 6 header.

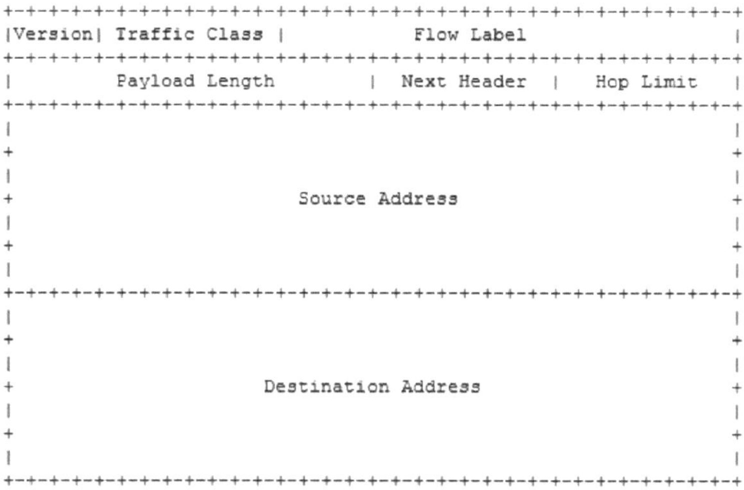

Source: Reproduced from RFC: 2460 - Internet Protocol, Version 6 (IPv6) Specification (IETF - Deering, S. and Hinden, R.; 1998).

Figure 6 shows the traditional Internet header in IPv6, requiring 40 octets or 40 bytes, i.e. 320 bits of information are added to the data segments to form datagrams which are normally fixed at 1280 bytes (Deering and Hinden, 1998). This sets the starting point for costs to increase by 3.125% over the total throughput. However, mixed networks, with both standards, are inevitable for a long time to come and are likely to always exist (Vanover, 2008), so these higher costs occur frequently and need to be taken into account, doubling the cost to around 6.94% (Oliveira *et al,* 2015 B).

These comparisons are shown in Figure 7, the evaluation is defined in terms of a basic cost per useful bit. The mixed implementation standard has a protocol overhead of 5 bits for every 72 bits of useful information, IPv6 needs one bit of overhead for every 32 bits, and IPv4 is set at 1 bit for every 29 bits of useful data. It should also be noted and emphasized that this comparison is relative to the typical increase in basic elementary cost for these encapsulation techniques in packet networks. (Oliveira *et al*, 2015 B)

Figure 7: Comparison of Internet Protocol Standards considering the basic cost per header bit and useful data.

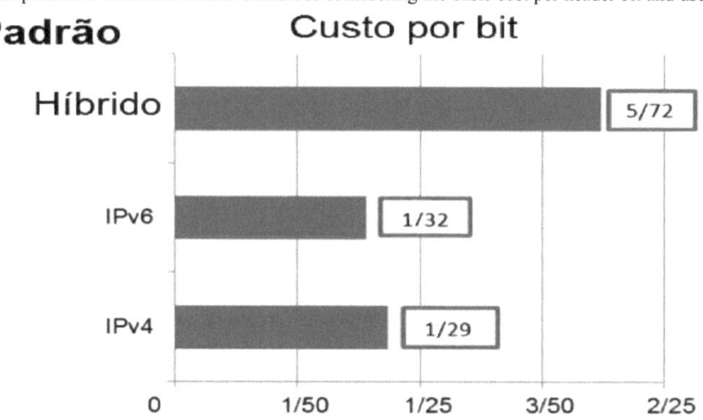

Source: Adapted and Reproduced from IP VIDEO DELIVERY COST: AN ANALYSIS...(OLIVEIRA *et al* ,2015 B)

4.1.2. TV Broadcast

Traditional television broadcasting has the same characteristics as a circuit-switched network: it is broadcast via bit streams, without segmentation, addressing, controls or encapsulation material (Bedicks, 2008). And, as well as being routed via an exclusive channel, it is a transmission that has a long history of availability and quality guarantees (Bedicks, 2008).

Furthermore, cable, satellite and terrestrial TV broadcasts are categorized as one-way communications, i.e. they do not need control mechanisms. Hence the association of video and audio to be distributed simply forces the end user's receiver to be positioned within range of a radio signal, for example, as long as there is an acceptable Signal-to-Noise-Ratio (SNR). (Oliveira *et al*, 2015 A; STOLFI, 2008; Shannon; 1948)

4.2. Software for measuring connection availability in a segregated manner

In order to carry out the availability assessment of an IP connection, a computer-programmed solution was designed that uses various software-based technologies. Starting with the development of the tool, the objectives that should be included in its architecture were listed: the use of open source programs, an integrated web environment, continuous logging and timestamping of tests, cross-platform hardware operation by the end user and the controlled user, and customizable evaluations. All these features were achieved by using the following materials and methods described.

4.2.1. Requirements Analysis

The software is centered on the Java programming language and developed on the open platform 'Spring Tool Suite 3.4.0 release' (Pivotal Software, 2015). This suite is coupled with the Eclipse IDE (Integrated Development Environment), which offered a coherent set of tools suitable for the intended project. This suite has what can be called the coding core of the program. The most relevant parts of this code are described in the next section. In addition to coding, it is important to mention the connections with the database and the web server. Two of these are functional associations with a relational database management system (RDBMS) and a web server. The RDBMS, the program used to store the evaluation reports, was 'MySQL 6.0 Community Edition' (Oracle Corporation, 2015). This is a database system that uses Structured Query Language (SQL) to manage and manipulate information. While the Web Server chosen, working as a path for communication with the Internet and acting together to deliver a browser interface, was 'Apache Tomcat 7.0.50' (Tomcat, 2015). This designated trio operates simultaneously. In order to efficiently understand how this program works, a step-by-step explanation of the finished software is shown below in the foreground, i.e. the user interface, and in the background, i.e. the coded algorithms and their tables.

4.2.2. Development

The development of the software resulted in the initial interface shown in Figure 8, which can be accessed via any web browser, once the software has been installed and the Apache Tomcat server is automatically connected and activated as local service 47. Then enter 'http://localhost:8080/ping' or 'http://127.0.0.1:8080/ping' in the address field. The 'localhost' or '127.0.0.1' indicates that it is a local service physically installed on the user's machine. The '8080' is a well-known TCP port for Web servers (Tomcat, 2015). And 'ping' is an address alias specified for the software and also a reminder for the network utility used in this application (Microsoft, 2015). And, for the example referred to in Figure 8, it is using 'Mozilla Firefox 29.0' (Mozilla, 2015).

In addition, Figure 8 offers ten specifications of *Uniform Resource Locators* URLs, or resource locators, which are selections to be checked over several possible time allocations, as well as choosing the number of tests desired. These different URL options allow any number of numerical IP addresses or literal DNS (*Domain Name System*) addresses to be tested. In computer networks, IP and DNS are responsible for locating a required resource, i.e. data (Tanenbaum & Wetherall, 2010; Ross and Kurose, 2013). It should be noted that, on the World Wide Web, data is generally kept on a website. Therefore, testing whether a URL is available consistently and continuously takes on increased importance. Especially when the most accessed websites on the Internet offer media content, i.e. music and/or video (TECHNAVIO, 2014; Ofcom, 2014).

The home page of the example application (Figure 8) brings together all the optional fields already filled in with a range of options already selected and filled in by the user, which are the parameters. These options start at the top of the screen between URLs 1 and 10. Next, the number of times this series of addresses will be tested is quantified in the 'Number of Repetitions' field to configure the number of repetitions. Below, there are two selectable timings. The first is the time between each complete set of tests, in milliseconds (ms), labeled 'Interval between sets of tests (ms)', which is the interval between sets of tests (ms). The second refers to the milliseconds to be waited after each single URL scan, labeled 'Interval between each ping (ms)' referring to the interval between each ping (ms). After that, a 'Save' button has the function of subscribing to investigations and activating tests. It also provides a confirmation message confirming that the request is actually in the processing queue. Finally, just below is another button, acting as a link for the program to display the next page. It is colored in blue letters and is labeled "View Ping Tests and Reports" to view the Ping Tests and Reports. This page is shown in Figure 9 and includes the analysis results sent to be processed from this home page in Figure 8.

Figure 8: Home page of the Availability Benchmarking Software with examples of website URLs and other settings filled in, accessed via the Firefox browser.

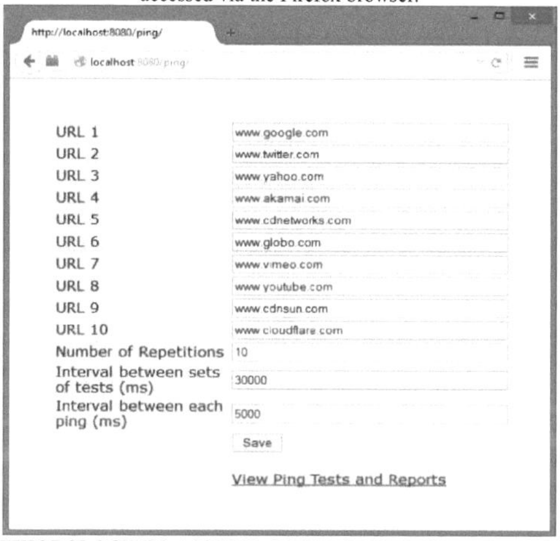

Source: Reproduced from METHODOLOGY TO ASSES IP CONNECTION...(OLIVEIRA *et al*,2015 A)

The application screen illustrated in Figure 9 shows an information table that fully reports each series and state of the defined tests. Thus, as soon as the record button in Figure 8 is clicked, what is configured in the URL fields together with the other specifications are sent to start execution according to a queue line. This is a priority list provided on the basis of the sequencing structure time. In this way, the set saved the first time the user sends it receives an identification or ID, numbered 1, and the next sets of get an ID of base n+1, i.e. last number of the ID + 1, a mathematical formula occurs for each new series of web addresses arranged to be checked. This feature is in the first column of the first table, designated on the top left-hand side as ID, where it can be read from bottom to top from oldest to newest. In addition, a record of the time of this queuing procedure is captured and placed in the sixth column of the top table, from left to right. It is named Date/Time, describing
Day/Month/Year and Hours:Minutes:Seconds as time indication. Continuing in the same table at the top of the next image, there are several columns: ID, Status, Repetitions, Interval between sets of tests (ms), Interval between each ping (ms), Date/Time and Actions. All of these have been previously described except status and actions.

Regarding the rows in the 'Status' column, it is necessary to explain that it indicates the status of the registered tests displayed in the interface in Figure 8. In this way, it tells you whether a queued request is in one of five possible conditions: 'Processed Successfully' for Successfully Processed, 'Aborted' for Aborted Process, 'Aborting' for Aborting Process, 'Processing' for Processing or 'Waiting to Start Processing' for Waiting to Start Processing. Processed successfully indicates that the evaluations have finished without any setbacks. Aborted is shown when the user has terminated the checks before their completion. Aborting means the same thing, but it is displayed while closure is currently in progress. Processing says that ping investigations are in progress, i.e. currently taking place on the user's device. To conclude, Waiting to start processing is a status before the last one described, it shows that the selected configurations are on hold, waiting to start executing once the others finish or are aborted. Meanwhile, the Actions column presents up to two possible options via links: 'List' to list and 'Stop' to Stop. The 'List' link reveals the bottom table in Figure 9, which details the test results for that row, or ID. 'Stop' is used to cease the ongoing evaluation of that particular ID, because once clicked, it causes the tests to be canceled and, immediately after being activated, an abort and/or aborted status is shown for it. In addition, there is another link in blue letters that should be noted, with the title: 'Schedule Tests'. It is a navigation link to the first page of the program (Figure 8), allowing the user to include more test sets, even while other(s) are running. This analysis allows the inclusion of specific analyses of the availability of advertising and other services offered by a DNS.

Figure 9: Results Exploration Page with Examples of Availability Benchmarking Software Tests accessed via the Firefox browser.

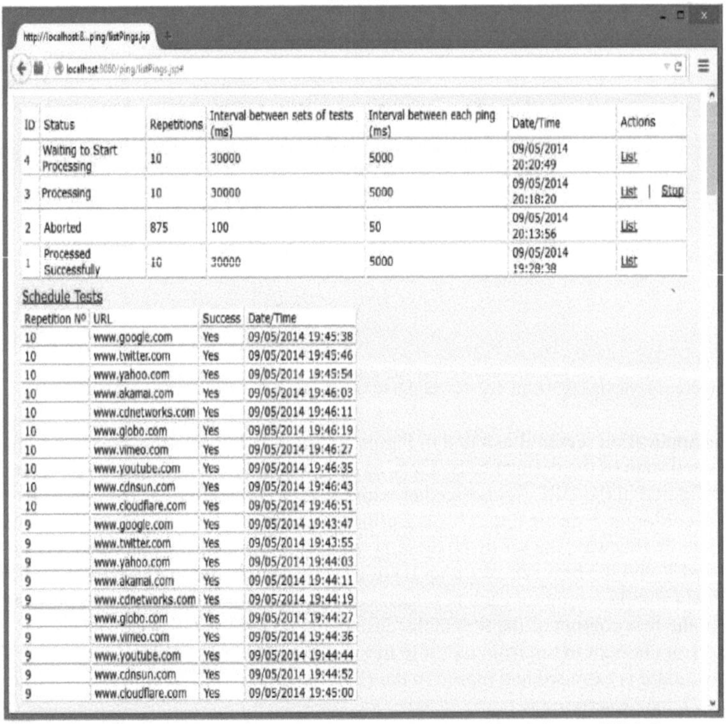

http://localhost:8...ping/listPings.jsp

localhost:8080/ping/listPings.jsp#

ID	Status	Repetitions	Interval between sets of tests (ms)	Interval between each ping (ms)	Date/Time	Actions
4	Waiting to Start Processing	10	30000	5000	09/05/2014 20:20:49	List
3	Processing	10	30000	5000	09/05/2014 20:18:20	List | Stop
2	Aborted	875	100	50	09/05/2014 20:13:56	List
1	Processed Successfully	10	30000	5000	09/05/2014 19:28:38	List

Schedule Tests

Repetition Nº	URL	Success	Date/Time
10	www.google.com	Yes	09/05/2014 19:45:38
10	www.twitter.com	Yes	09/05/2014 19:45:46
10	www.yahoo.com	Yes	09/05/2014 19:45:54
10	www.akamai.com	Yes	09/05/2014 19:46:03
10	www.cdnetworks.com	Yes	09/05/2014 19:46:11
10	www.globo.com	Yes	09/05/2014 19:46:19
10	www.vimeo.com	Yes	09/05/2014 19:46:27
10	www.youtube.com	Yes	09/05/2014 19:46:35
10	www.cdnsun.com	Yes	09/05/2014 19:46:43
10	www.cloudflare.com	Yes	09/05/2014 19:46:51
9	www.google.com	Yes	09/05/2014 19:43:47
9	www.twitter.com	Yes	09/05/2014 19:43:55
9	www.yahoo.com	Yes	09/05/2014 19:44:03
9	www.akamai.com	Yes	09/05/2014 19:44:11
9	www.cdnetworks.com	Yes	09/05/2014 19:44:19
9	www.globo.com	Yes	09/05/2014 19:44:27
9	www.vimeo.com	Yes	09/05/2014 19:44:36
9	www.youtube.com	Yes	09/05/2014 19:44:44
9	www.cdnsun.com	Yes	09/05/2014 19:44:52
9	www.cloudflare.com	Yes	09/05/2014 19:45:00

Source: Reproduced from METHODOLOGY TO ASSES IP CONNECTION...(OLIVEIRA *et al*,2015 A)

The contents of the bottom table in Figure 9 are divided into four columns to display the availability checks for each IP or DNS. Starting from the left side to the right side, you see 'Repetition N°' for 'Repetition N°', 'URL', 'Success' to indicate the success or failure of the test and 'Date/Time' for Date/Time. The first marks the number of tests at each URL. After it is the DNS or IP, also marked as the Uniform Resource Locator. Next, the 'Success' column is present, with information on whether or not the URL was available at that time for the specific repetition. This result is given as a yes (Yes) or no (No) answer. Next to this is the date and time for each link analysis result, it carries the same pattern of recording the date/time as the top table.

To complete the materials and methods used in the development of this solution, it is essential to expose the core programming of the software. And, since it is recognized that the ping procedure is the core of the program, its commented coding as it is typed within the 'Spring Tool Suite' is shown in Figure 10. It shows the java code that contains the customized routine for using the 'ping' network utility separately and capturing its results for each URL. Specifically, some adapted parameters that come with this network utility tool (ping) are noted. These are '-n 1' and 'w 2000', representing, respectively, the total of one echo request for packets sent and 2000 milliseconds of waiting time for their reply. After the ping acts by fetching the URL, the system captures a true or false attribute that is stored in a binary (1 or 0) pattern in the database, which will later be displayed as a Yes or No in the user's success column (Figure 9) on the Explore Page. In addition, there is another scenario that inserts an extra 3000 milliseconds for the ping to be triggered. This time window is included as a fail-safe measure because it gives the system enough time to process the pings, store the data in the MySQL table and place it in the software's user interface. This prevents processing requests from accumulating and/or blocking the software, even when the computer is under excessive use or when the user needs direct, continuous and repetitive tests with zero time set in the interval between each (ms) ping field. This also ensures that the software does not take up a significant part of the hardware processing time on the device where it is installed. This also guarantees low network bandwidth consumption.

Figure 10: Method for pinging URLs and capturing the results - Java coding for IP connection availability checking software.

```
// Method to ping URLs and capture the results
    public static boolean runPing(String ipstr) {
        boolean retv = false;
        try {
            InputStream ins = Runtime.getRuntime()
// Invokes the execution of ping against a URL address (ipstr)
//sending 1 echo request( -n 1) and waiting 2000 milliseconds(-w 2000) for its response
                    .exec("ping -n 1 -w 2000 " + ipstr).getInputStream();
// Makes the program wait (sleep) for 3000 milliseconds
            Thread.sleep(3000);
//Captures the response and saves the true or false response
            byte[] prsbuf = new byte[ins.available()];
            ins.read(prsbuf);
            String parsstr = new StringTokenizer(new String(prsbuf), "%")
                    .nextToken().trim();
            if (!parsstr.endsWith("100") && !parsstr.endsWith("again."))
                retv = true;
        } catch (Exception e) {
            retv = false;
        }
// Returns the result of the URL's ping
//that will later be shown as a Yes or No information in the Success column
        return retv;
    }
}
```

Source: Reproduced from METHODOLOGY TO ASSES IP CONNECTION...(OLIVEIRA *et al* ,2015 A)

As soon as the ping tests are run, two key tables within a MySQL database system are populated, i.e. filled with the test requests and results. These are called 'queue', to indicate the table with the queue of test battery requests, and 'ping_log', which is the table that stores the captured results. These tables are shown in Figures 11 and 12. The 'queue' table, considered in Figure 11, records the required availability request as soon as the 'Save' button (Figure 8) is pressed. Thus, the main parts of the detailed information requests are stored in a row in this table. That is, both the timings ('interval_milisecs' and 'interval_ping_milisecs') and the number of repetitions ('repeat_num') are stored in it. In addition, it holds the time ('create_timestamp') at which the requests were sent, as well as the current state of the handling ('status'). This distinction is reflected in the previously described 'Status' column on the page containing Exploration of the interface (Figure 9). In addition, it is worth noting the assignment of a 'queue_id', which numerically organizes the order of events per line, i.e. in a queue of requests.

Figure 11: Availability queue table, captured and adapted from MySQL Workbench.
Source: Reproduced from METHODOLOGY TO ASSES IP CONNECTION...(OLIVEIRA *et al* ,2015 A)

	queuejd	status	repeatjium	interval_milisecs	interval_pina_milisecs	createjimestamp
	1	PROCESSED	10	30000	500D	09/05/2014 19:23:38
	2	ABORTED	875	100	50	09/05/2014 20:13:56
	3	PROCESSING	10	30000	500D	09/05/2014 20:13:20
	4	PENDING	10	30000	5000	09/05/2014 20:20:49

As for the other table emphasized, called 'ping_log', its most notable role is to continuously record test results. In Figure 12 the ping responses are corroborated by the 'successful' column, if it displays 1 it means that the Uniform Resource Locator was available at that exact moment corresponding also to the information present in the 'create_timestamp' column and, if it is 0, this is an indication of unavailability. It also keeps the related retry number ('repeat_id'), the verified URL ('url') and the requested queue ID ('queue_id'). To conclude, in the top left corner of this table there is a 'ping_log_id' providing an arithmetic sequence starting at 1 at the beginning and systematically adding 1 to the next line of information about the next test run.

Figure 12: Availability table 'ping_log' (row), captured and adapted from MySQL Workbench.
Source: Reproduced from METHODOLOGY TO ASSES IP CONNECTION...(OLIVEIRA *et al* ,2015 A)

	pingjogjdqueuejd		repeatjd	url	successful	createjimestamp
	1	1	1	www.google.com	1	09/05/2014 19:29:00
	2	1	1	www.twitter.com	1	09/05/2014 19:29:08

	3	1	1	www.yahoo.com	1	09/05/2014 19:29:16
	4	1	1	www.akamai.com	1	09/05/2014 19:29:24
	5	1	1	www .cdnetworks .com	1	09/05/2014 19:29:32
	G	1	1	www.globo.com	1	09/05/2014 19:29:40
	7	1	1	www.vimeo.com	1	09/05/2014 19:29 48
	8	1	1	www.youtube.com	1	09/05/2014 19:29:56
	8	1	1	**www.cdnsun.com**	1	09/05/2014 19:30:04
	10	1	1	www .cloudflane.com	1	09/05/2014 19:30:12
		111	2	www.google.com	1	09/05/2014 19:30:51
	12	1	2	www.twitter.com	1	09/05/2014 19:30:59
	13	1	2	www.yahoo.com	1	09/05/201419:31:07
	14	1	2	www.akamai.com	1	09/05/201419:31:15
	15	1	2	www .cdnetworks .com	1	09/05/201419:31:23
	16	1	2	www.globo.com	1	09/05/201419:31:31

	17	1	2	www.vimeo.com	1	09/05/201419:31:39
	18	1	2	www.youtube.com	1	09/05/201419:31:47

4.3 Software for Audience Capture Associated with Video Stream Availability

4.3.1. Requirements Analysis

As for the Video Stream Audience Capture Software, a solution was designed taking into account the aforementioned importance of obtaining information at the user's end about videos delivered via IP from the Internet's largest online media provider, i.e. YouTube (Statista, 2015A; Statista, 2016). In addition, the application must be compatible with one of the most widely used browsers today, Google Chrome (Statista, 2015 B). Considering the requirements, in order to capture the audience of audiovisual content, we decided on a project in which the program should consist of two parts, described below.

The client side, or Front-end, is an application to be installed in the *browser* in extension format that could be installed on any device with the extension-enabled Google Chrome browser. It collects and sends certain data to a centralizer. This data is statistics (measurements and information) of videos accessed, i.e. viewed by users. It should be noted that this is done on the basis of data present in the site's public code when a page with a YouTube video is accessed, at which point the application becomes active. The data selected to be captured and sent automatically to the centralizer is:

- Total time the page is open;

This variable was chosen to assess how long a user is willing to stay on a page to view content, which is associated with both audience and availability.

- Time to load the video;

This parameter is used to measure the initial availability for the content to be viewed.

- Time of video watched;

This metric demonstrates the strong relationship with the audience, as it denotes how long the content has been played.

- Time with video in Pause;

This time is closely related to the issue of content availability and the audience, as it shows how long a user is willing to wait for content to be viewed. In addition, it allows for more in-depth analysis and opens up the possibility that other possibilities may have occurred, such as the user pausing the video for it to load, or pausing it out of sheer forgetfulness when accessing other content, or pausing it too long to load the intended content. - Total Video Time;

This metric is necessary to compare how long that video has been watched.

- Number of Interactions in the *Timeline*, i.e. during the video's duration bar;

This number gives us clues as to availability, because if a user has had to interact with the content many times, this is something relevant to observe. It also touches on the question of audience in case a person wants to watch the same video or excerpt several times.

- Post-video time;

This variable, combined with the total time, helps to separate out the time spent on that video, as well as delimiting the question of availability, since this time can be used to pre-load the next video if the person has some kind of automatic playback activated;

- URL, *Universal Resource Locator,* i.e. the Internet address of the video;

Knowing which content is or isn't available, whether or not it has a satisfactory audience, is necessary for the commercial chain involved in IP delivery.

- View, number of views and, consequently, the number of the specific view;

This metric proves to be necessary to observe, as it contributes to the strategy of the CDN and others to pre-load the content demanded, thus meeting the expectations of the ecosystem in question.

- Channel, i.e. the producer and/or owner of the content;

Knowing the channel is interesting because it lets you know that even if a piece of content doesn't have many views on this platform, it may have high demand on another provider (e.g. consolidated TV and radio channels and programs, Facebook pages of digital influencers, etc.) and this should be noted.

- Subscribers, i.e. the number of users subscribed to the Channel;

This number values the number of people who will be contacted if the channel releases a new video, so if the channel has a lot of subscribers it's usually because its audience is high, which affects the providers' strategy for availability.

In addition, other data deemed relevant is captured through a brief questionnaire to be filled in by the user when the software is installed. These are:

- City;

Knowing the user's physical location helps a lot in evaluating the connection, since QoS is subjective. This can help with CDN strategy issues (e.g. a user accessing from a metropolis versus a user accessing from a remote region).

- Age;

Since the shift from traditional TV to Internet "TV" is generational, i.e. the younger the person, the greater the demand for network content, the more availability they expect. - Sex.

Since YouTube video access is 68% male and 32% female (Statistic Brain, 2016; Youtube, 2017), we need to know which part of the captured data base we need to increase. That is, if we need more users and of which gender.

In addition, all the data has a time stamp so that it can be analyzed separately, for example when a piece of content premieres. Furthermore, all the information captured and the respective analyses are in chapters 5.3.2.1 and 5.3.2.2.

The part of the centralizer, or server that receives, stores, manipulates and displays all this data, is called the Back-end. This is software that acts as a server on the Internet, which will provide services for receiving, saving (logging) and querying the captured data, segmenting it into database tables.

1.3.1.1. Modeling with UML - Unified Modeling *Language*

In the requirements analysis stage, it was necessary to model the intended solution. The aim was to design the relationship between coding, database, processes involved and communication based on the premises of the UML - *Unified* Modeling Language. There are several definitions for this method, but for the purposes of this project the one considered was the concept of system design via a diagram as proposed in its generic premises (Arthemia, 2017; Object Management Group (OMG), 2017; Alhir, 2003). Figure 13 below illustrates this diagram. It seeks to elucidate the functioning of the system entities in question.

Figure 13 UML diagram of the represented solution.

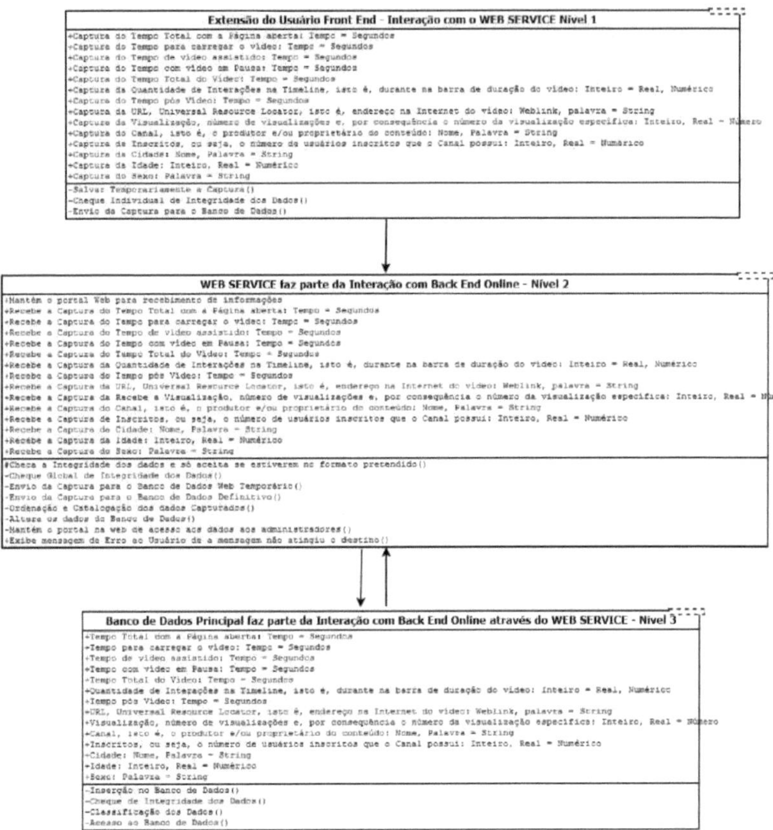

Source: Own figure

13.3.2. Development

In order to develop software capable of interacting with Youtube's so-called API (Application Programming Interface), we chose the JavaScript language. the JavaScript language was selected. And to store the data, we used a MySQL database and, consequently, the SQL language to manipulate and process the data. Below are the main parts of the coding implemented for the Front- end, which is the extension installed in the browser of the audiovisual content consumer's device.

Figure 14 shows the programming of a code that checks for changes to the page, i.e. the URL address, and records it, saving the data locally whenever a change to another page is made. In other words, it captures when the user stops accessing certain content and saves all the information monitored and captured in browser cookies on the client machine.

Figure 14: Coding of the Extension with the functions for checking URL updates and/or browser output and sending data to the local database.

```
//VERIFICA SE O USUARIO ATUALIZOU OU VAI SAIR DO BROWNSER
var allowPrompt = true;
$(document).click(function(event) {
    allowPrompt = true;
});

$(document).ready(function() {
    window.onbeforeunload = WarnUser;
});

function WarnUser() {
    if(allowPrompt) {
        //ENVIA DADOS PARA O BANCO
        SetData("");
        return ".";
    } else {
        SetData("");
        allowPrompt = true;
        if (localStorage.clickcount) {
            localStorage.clickcount = Number(localStorage.clickcount) + 1;
        } else {
            localStorage.clickcount = 1;
        }
    }
}
```

Source: Own figure

Figure 15 shows a code programmed to check that the user's personal data has been filled in when they first use the Extension. In other words, as soon as the extension is installed in the browser and a page with YouTube videos is accessed, the following code asks the user to fill in their City, Age and Gender via a questionnaire. This questionnaire is filled in only once, on first use, after which this data is automatically stored in the browser's cookies. You can also see from this code that this information is configured to be mandatory, and is programmed so that the user does not skip or fail to fill in this information.

Figure 15: Coding of the Extension to check if the data that the user needs to fill in at the time of the first use has been answered.

```
//VERIFICA SE O USUARIO JÁ PREENCHEU ALGUNS DADOS SOLICITADOS;
function SetDataUser(){
    //Verifica se o campo Cidade está preenchido
    if (localStorage.getItem('cidadeUsuario') == null) {
        var cidadeUsuario =
prompt("Youbute Stats v1.0, \n\nVamos coletar algumas informacoes:\n\nInforme sua cidade:", "São Paulo")
        if (cidadeUsuario != null) {
            localStorage.cidadeUsuario = cidadeUsuario;
            localStorage.setItem('cidadeUsuario', cidadeUsuario);
        } else {
            alert('O campo Cidade deve ser preenchido!');
        }
    }
    //Verifica se o campo Idade está preenchido
    if (localStorage.getItem('ageUsuario') == null) {
        var ageUsuario = prompt("Informe sua idade:");
        if (ageUsuario != null) {
            localStorage.ageUsuario = ageUsuario;
            localStorage.setItem('ageUsuario', ageUsuario);
        } else {
            alert('O campo Idade deve ser preenchido!');
        }
    }
    //Verifica se o campo Sexo está preenchido
    if (localStorage.getItem('sexoUsuario') == null) {
        var sexoUsuario = prompt("Informe seu sexo:", "M ou F");
        if (sexoUsuario != null) {
            localStorage.sexoUsuario = sexoUsuario;
            localStorage.setItem('sexoUsuario', sexoUsuario);
        } else {
            alert('O campo Sexo deve ser preenchido!');
        }
    }
}
```

Source: Own figure

The main coding, called the core programming of the Extension, is shown in Figure 16 below. From the comment "//COLLECT VIDEO INFORMATION" you can see the existing interaction with the YouTube API. This is the coding that was the most difficult to discover and implement, especially the time information contained in the script, which changes over time, i.e. during the playback of a video. In it, we collect the name of the video, time watched, total time, number of views and number of subscribers to the channel. Prior to this, we have this information defined as variables in this larger function, which has the purpose of recording the data in the Back-End. Immediately after collecting the data, we have the function that forwards all this data to a web service maintained by the website configured for this purpose on the domain owned by the company, 'tetconsultoria.com.br'. If the communication fails to send this data, the user is sent a message about this problem stating that the web service was not communicated with and was unavailable to send the data.

Figure 16: Coded core of the Extension demonstrating the capture of monitored data and sending it to the web server's back-end.

```
//COLETA INFORMACOES DO VIDEO
$(document).ready(function() {
    nomeVideo = $('.watch-title').text();
    var element = $('.ytp-progress-bar');
    if (element.length > 0) {
        $(element[0].attributes).each(function () {
            if (this.nodeName == 'aria-valuenow') {                    tempoAssistido = this.nodeValue;  }
            else if (this.nodeName == 'aria-valuemax') {               tempoTotal = this.nodeValue;}});}
    numeroVisualizacao = $('.watch-view-count').text();  nomeCanal = $('.yt-user-info').text();   numeroInscrito = $('.yt-subscriber-count').text();});
arrayAssistido += ',' + tempoContador + '-' + tempoAssistido + '-' + new Date().getDate() + '/' + new Date().getMonth() + '/' + new Date().getFullYear() +
                                                    + new Date().getHours() + ':' + new Date().getMinutes() + ':' + new Date().getSeconds()
 console.log("URL - ", window.location.href);   console.log("---------");
 closeWindow = new Date().getTime();    openTime = (closeWindow - openWindow) / 1000;    tempoCarrega = (tempoCarrega - openWindow) / 1000;
 if (tempoTotal != "0"){
    //ENVIA DADOS PARA O WEBSERVICE
    $.ajax({            type: "POST",
        url: 'https://www.tetconsultoria.com.br/WS.asmx/SetStats4',
        data: "{ nomeVideo:'" + nomeVideo.trim() + "',"+
            "  tempoAssistido:'" + tempoContador + "',"+
            "  tempoTotal:'" + tempoTotal + "',"+
            "  urlVideo:'" + urlPlay + "',"+
            "  numeroVisualizacao:'" + numeroVisualizacao + "',"+
            "  nomeCanal:'" + nomeCanal.trim() + "',"+
            "  numeroInscrito:'" + numeroInscrito + "',"+
            "  cidadeUsuario:'" + localStorage.getItem('cidadeUsuario') + "',"+
            "  idadeUsuario:'" + localStorage.getItem('ageUsuario') + "',"+
            "  sexoUsuario:'" + localStorage.getItem('sexoUsuario') + "'," +
            "  tempoPagina:'" + Math.round(openTime) + "'," +
            "  tempoPausa:'" + tempoPausado + "'," +
            "  tempoPosVideo:'" + tempoPosVideo + "'," +
            "  arrayAssistido:'" + arrayAssistido + "'," +
            "  tempoCarrega:'" + Math.round(tempoCarrega) + "'" +
            " }",
        contentType: "application/json; charset=utf-8",
        dataType: "json",
        success: function (msg) {           },
        error: function (e) {
            alert('Mensagem WS03 - webserivce unreachable');}      });
```

Source: Own figure

For the Extension and this software to work properly, a continuous check of which page the user is on, which page they have moved to, whether or not they have moved, etc. is necessary in order not to lose any content. This is because the information captured by the codes described above is captured and sent to the centralizer automatically for each video page accessed. In other words, there is a sequence of monitoring, capturing and sending to the WebService. In order to achieve this goal of checking for changes on the page, both to send the information already collected and to start a new collection, the methods shown in Figure 17 below were implemented. This code checks whether the URL has changed at the user's request, by automatic means from the YouTube site itself, when the automatic continuous playback of videos in sequence is configured on this site, since this is how it is by default on the site. Furthermore, as an additional check, the page is scanned every 100 milliseconds to see if it has changed. This coding triggers the sending of all information as soon as a change occurs, and it is only at this moment of change that it is sent.

Figure 17: Coding of the Extension with functions to continuously check for changes on the user's page.

```
(function( ) {    // VERIFICA URL ATUAL
    var strLocation = window.location.href;
    var strHash = window.location.hash;
    var strPrevLocation = "";
    var strPrevHash = "";
    // Esta é a frequência com que serão checkint para
    // Mudanças no local
    var intIntervalTime = 100;
    // Esse método remove a libra a partir do hash .
    var fnCleanHash = function( strHash ){
        return(strHash.substring( 1, strHash.length ));    }
    //VERIFICA OS DADOS DO USUARIO
    SetDataUser();
    //YOUTUBE FAZ TRANSACAO DE PAGINAS DE DUAS FORMAS (INERNOS E EXTERNOS),
    //PARA LINKS INTERNOS UTILIZA AJAX E A CAPTURA DESSA
    //INFORMACAO É FEITA UTILIZANDO O CODIGO ABAIXO
    // Este será o método que usamos para verificar
    // Mudanças na localização da janela .
    var fnCheckLocation = function() {
        // Verifique se o local foi alterado.
        if (strLocation != window.location.href){
            //ENVIA DADOS QND CAPTURA MUDANCA DE PAGINA POR AJAX
            SetData("DENTRO");
            // Armazenar os locais novos e anteriores.
            strPrevLocation = strLocation;
            strPrevHash = strHash;
            strLocation = window.location.href;
            strHash = window.location.hash;
            // A localização mudou. gatilho um
            // Muda evento no objeto local ,
            // Passando o atual e anterior
            // Valores de localização .
            $( window.location ).trigger("change",{
                            currentHref: strLocation,
                            currentHash: fnCleanHash( strHash ),
                            previousHref: strPrevLocation,
                            previousHash: fnCleanHash( strPrevHash )  }); }  }
    // INFORMA um intervalo para verificar as mudanças de local .
    setInterval( fnCheckLocation, intIntervalTime );})( jQuery );
```

Source: Own figure

The Back-end programming part is illustrated in Figure 18. This shows the coding that implements the web server that accepts, receives and inserts the feedback, i.e. the information collected from all the videos accessed by all the users who have the client installed in their browser, into the SQL database. The programming demonstrates ASMX, or '*Active Server MethodFile*', which is the Web Service of the .NET language, the method implemented in this part of the solution that implements the page and provides the aforementioned server. Then there is the request that accesses the MySQL database and allocates all the data. This insertion defines the tabulation, parameterization in columns in a table created in the database for the information collected from customers.

Figure 18: Back-end coding with WebService programming to accept information from customers and save it in an SQL database.

```
using System;using System.Collections.Generic;using System.Linq;using System.Web; using System.Web.Services;
using System.Collections;using System.Web.Services.Protocols;using System.Web.Script.Services;using MySql.Data.MySqlClient;
//DEFINICAO DO WEBSERVICE
namespace WService {[WebService(Namespace = "https://www.tetconsultoria.com.br/ws.asmx/setstats1", Name = "WSExtension")]
    [WebServiceBinding(ConformsTo = WsiProfiles.BasicProfile1_1)] [System.ComponentModel.ToolboxItem(false)]
    //METODO CRIADO PARA O WEBSERVICE
    [System.Web.Script.Services.ScriptService] public class WS : System.Web.Services.WebService
 {[WebMethod] public string SetStats(string nomeVideo, string tempoAssistido, string tempoTotal, string urlVideo,
 string tempoCarrega, string tempoPausa, string numeroTransacoes,string numeroVisualizacao, string nomeCanal,
 string numeroInscrito, string cidadeUsuario, string idadeUsuario, string sexoUsuario)
        { string msg = ""; //ACESSO AO BANCO DE DADOS
using (MySqlConnection conexao = new MySqlConnection("Server=MYSQL5015.Smarterasp.net;Database=db_9f5aee_system;Uid=9f5aee_system;Pwd=banco123;"))
 {MySqlTransaction transacao; try {conexao.Open(); transacao = conexao.BeginTransaction();MySqlCommand command = new MySqlCommand();
command.Connection = conexao;command.Transaction = transacao;
//INSERT NO BANCO DE DADOS
command.CommandText = "INSERT INTO `db_9f5aee_system`.`youtubestats` (`ysNomeVideo`, `ysTempoCarrega`, `ysTempoPausa`, `ysNumeroTransacoes`, " +
 "`ysTempoAssistido`, `ysTempoTotal`, `ysUrlVideo`, `ysNumeroVisualizacao`, `ysNomeCanal`," +
 "`ysNumeroInscrito`, `ysCidadeUsuario`, `ysIdadeUsuario`, `ysSexoUsuario`, `ysData`) " +
"VALUES (@NomVideo, @TempoCarrega, @TempoPausa, @NumeroTransacoes, @TempoAssistido, @TempoTotal, @UrlVideo, @NumeroVisualizacao, @NomeCanal, " +
"@NumeroInscrito, @CidadeUsuario, @IdadeUsuario, @SexoUsuario, now());";
                    command.Prepare();                          //PARAMETROS
                    command.Parameters.AddWithValue("@NomVideo", nomeVideo);
                    command.Parameters.AddWithValue("@TempoCarrega", tempoCarrega);
                    command.Parameters.AddWithValue("@TempoPausa", tempoPausa);
                    command.Parameters.AddWithValue("@NumeroTransacoes", numeroTransacoes);
                    command.Parameters.AddWithValue("@TempoAssistido", tempoAssistido);
                    command.Parameters.AddWithValue("@TempoTotal", tempoTotal);
                    command.Parameters.AddWithValue("@UrlVideo", urlVideo);
                    command.Parameters.AddWithValue("@NumeroVisualizacao", numeroVisualizacao);
                    command.Parameters.AddWithValue("@NomeCanal", nomeCanal);
                    command.Parameters.AddWithValue("@NumeroInscrito", numeroInscrito);
                    command.Parameters.AddWithValue("@CidadeUsuario", cidadeUsuario);
                    command.Parameters.AddWithValue("@IdadeUsuario", idadeUsuario);
                    command.Parameters.AddWithValue("@SexoUsuario", sexoUsuario);
                    command.ExecuteNonQuery();transacao.Commit(); transacao.Dispose();
}catch (Exception ex){msg = "Falha ao salvar dados, " + msg;}
finally{conexao.Close();}} msg = "Salvo com sucesso."; return msg;}}}
```

Source: Own figure

Figure 19 shows this categorization of data within the RDBMS used, or Relational Database. In this image you can see how the data categorization fits into the appropriate fields, or rather columns, of the table where the data received by the Back-end is stored. It's worth noting that the data structure is being visualized using an administrative tool called phpMyadmin.

Figure 19 Page for viewing the structure of the data in the MySQL table accessed via the phpMyAdmin administrative tool.

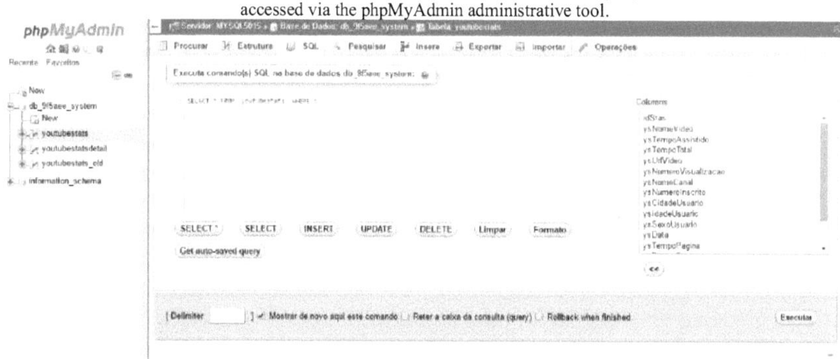

Source: Own figure

Figure 20 below shows, within the aforementioned administrative interface, the selection of the table that saves the data for display in the interface produced by the Back-end system for viewing all the information present in the database.

Figure 20: Display page for selecting the data in the MySQL table via the phpMyAdmin administrative tool.

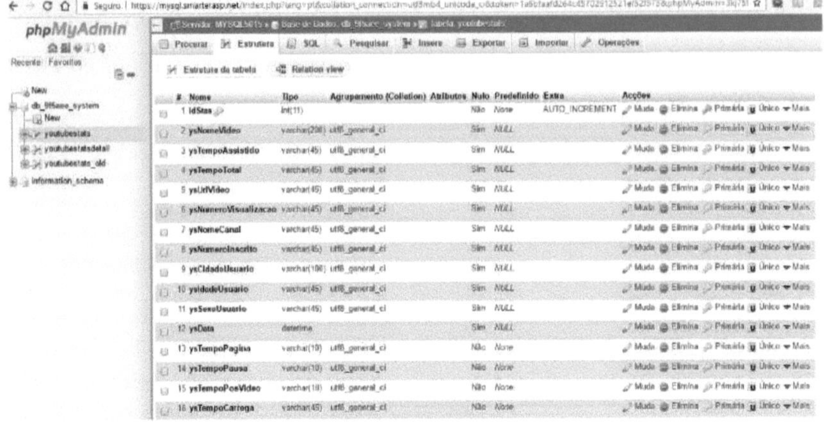

Source: Own figure

Figure 21 below also shows the administrative interface, a

example of searching for all the data in the table to be displayed in the interface produced by the back-end system to visualize all the information in the database. This user interface, which was largely implemented by the codes mentioned above, can be found in the results chapter on this software solution.

Figure 21: Search view page for the data in the MySQL table accessed via the phpMyAdmin administrative tool.

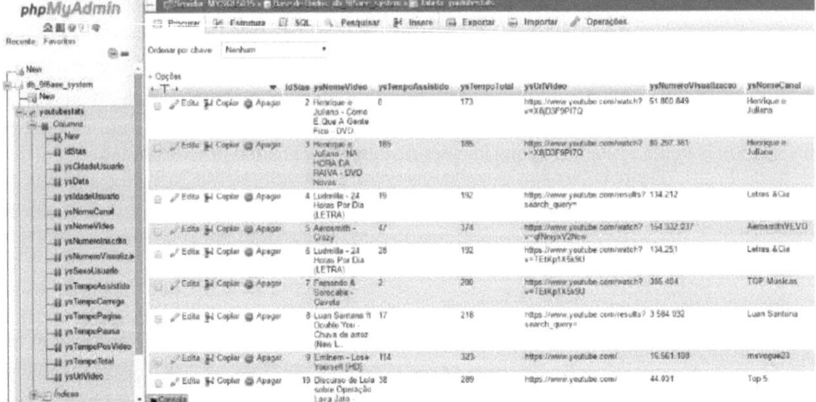

Source: Own figure

In addition, it is necessary to emphasize a point about this communication, data, attributes and parameters. The Back-end only accepts data that is sent with the attributes exactly as described in the codes presented; anything outside these parameters is not accepted by the WebService. In this way, the obligation to use the correct attributes guarantees the integrity and objectivity of the data and correct tabulation in the temporary storage in the client's cookies and in the correct record on the server side that receives the information.

Chapter 5

5. RESULTS

In this chapter, the products and/or deliverables of the four studies, analyses and implementations carried out are demonstrated.

5.1. Technical-Mathematical Comparison IP Stream versus TV Broadcast

The central challenges of broadcasting via Internet Protocol, i.e. IP Television (IPTV), are: sustaining bidirectional communication with the previously described control devices and duplicating information for each final destination device. To deal with this issue, Content Delivery Networks (CDNs) have proven to be reasonably successful for content that has already been recorded, i.e. not for live broadcasts. For live content, however, they cannot be properly applied, since the transmission is directly from the source to all the clients who request it. Such events can create a stressful environment, so almost all network bandwidth is quickly exhausted. (Oliveira *et al*, 2015 A; ITU, 2003, Kaduoka *et al,* 2016)

5.1.1. Cost in throughput and technical solution for live and non-live transmissions

Considering live broadcasts, a Full HD video plus audio stream, for a wide 16:9 screen and images up to 1920*1080 pixels in size, requires a throughput of around 19.3 Mbits per second on most digital TV standards in use today (Bedicks, 2008). And, considering the intrinsic packaging protocols for over the internet distribution (IPTV), this cost starts at 19.97 Mbits/sec for one user. Therefore, if the number of users increases this transfer rate follows a proportional and arithmetic linear growth. In other words, along with it, for two users it costs twice as much (39.94 Mbits/sec), for three it costs three times as much (59.91 Mbits/sec) and so on. It's important to bear in mind that traditional digital TV transmission only needs the initial bandwidth, which is continuously at 19.3 Mbits/sec. Figures 22, 23 and 24 show this mathematical evaluation graphically, where you can see the throughput for each choice and understand the reasons why a live IP stream is generally and correctly expected to become a cord-cutting incident.

This *throughput* cost, which is linear but in particular interpretations in the literature is considered to be exponential, is, until now, inevitable in IP networks, and any event for numerous clients is generally predicted, and subsequently confirmed, as an event called *'cord-cutters'*, which cause the transmission to malfunction or drop out altogether (Cloonan and Allen, 2011; Oliveira *et al,* 2015 A, Chaves de Oliveira *et al,* 2016 Kaduoka *et al, 2016*). Meanwhile, although TV is not an on-demand medium and users are directly involved in broadcasters' content decisions, it remains cost-effective, in terms of link utilization and technical feasibility, and is the choice for live broadcasts (Bedicks, 2008; Oliveira *et al,* 2015 A; Oliveira *et al*, 2015 B).

Figure 22: Comparison of the basic throughput of a Full HD IPTV Stream versus the number of users.

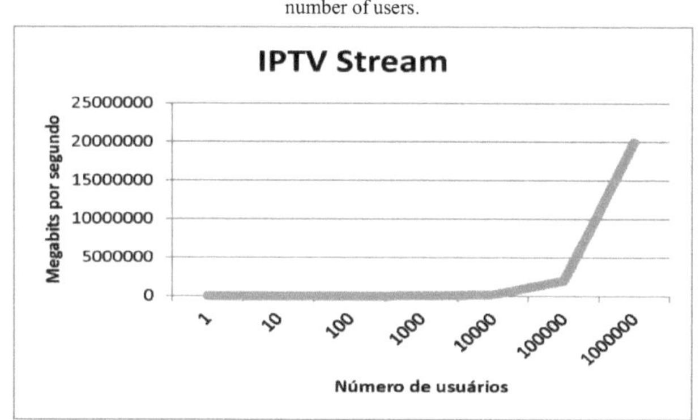

Source: Adapted and Reproduced from IP VIDEO DELIVERY COST: AN ANALYSIS...(OLIVEIRA *et al* ,2015 B)

Figure 23 Comparison of the basic throughput of a Full HD data stream in Traditional

Digital Television Broadcast versus the number of users.

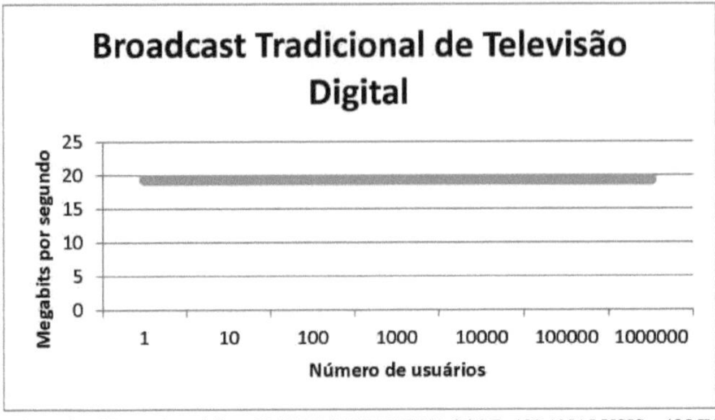

Source: Adapted and Reproduced from IP VIDEO DELIVERY COST: AN ANALYSIS... (OLIVEIRA *et al* ,2015 B)

Figure 24: Comparison of throughput for Full HD live streaming between IPTV and DTV.

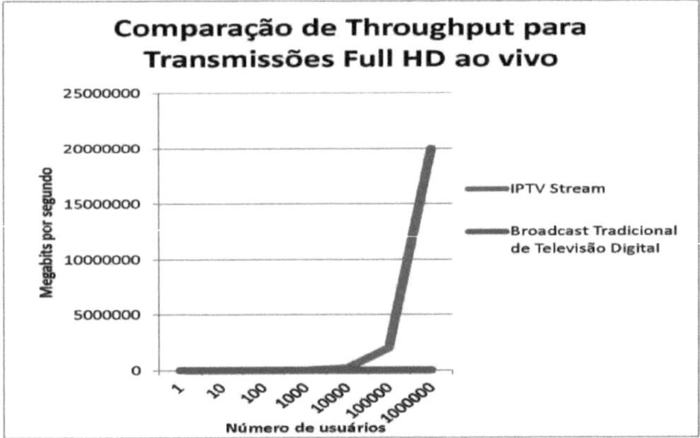

Source: Adapted and Reproduced from IP VIDEO DELIVERY COST: AN ANALYSIS...(OLIVEIRA *et al* ,2015 B)

In analysis, since today's landscape demands high definition for any and all media, it is necessary to evaluate the cost of making the choice to deliver content. Packet networks are inevitable, but by definition they do not offer guarantees of transmission and quality, requiring effective and well-planned approaches such as Content Delivery Networks to function properly for this purpose. However, to avoid their weak point, i.e. excessive streaming, live HD broadcasts need to either guarantee sufficient bandwidth for the task or limit numerous viewers. On the other hand, we have a proven technology, Digital Television, with recent improvements and which is, in terms of bitrate consumption, much more viable than any IP technique we have available today. This is an approach that is more likely to be successful, because on the one hand internet channel clogging is avoided and quality assurance is provided, serving countless customers in the high quality content standards they expect.

5.2. Software for Measuring Connection Availability in a Segregated Manner

5.2.1 Operation and Data Captured

When considering the design and captures of the Connection Availability Measurement Software, using the data provided in the tables in Figures 11 and 12, a line graph of the availability time must be designed, similar to a network connection assessment similar to the one shown in Figure 2, as well as to calculate an Experimentally Measured Full Network Availability (EMFNA, Equation 4). In this way, the expected results of the software application appear, i.e. the methodology for assessing the availability of the IP connection is achieved. By plotting the graph of the 'ping_log' table, it becomes clear to see how available the device's Internet connection was over a short period of just over two minutes, for the sake of illustration. Thus, in Figure 12, starting on 09/May/2014 at 19h29m00s and lasting until 19h31m47s on the same day, all 18 measurements taken through ping checks are emphasized and established over time, or 167 seconds. In this, a positive availability of 100% is seen, of zero seconds unavailable, for the period considered, which is also calculated by the EMFNA formula. Equation 5 (Oliveira *et al*,2015 A) defines how to compute the values for this measurement.

$$\textbf{Ping\_log}\ \text{EMFNA}\ (\%) = 1 - \frac{0\ \text{seconds}}{167\ \text{seconds}}\ (\text{x}100) = \mathbf{100\%} \qquad (5)$$

The following graph in Figure 25 confirms this calculation and displays the last two columns on the right of the 'ping_log' table: 'successful' and 'create_timestamp'. This is the reason for the time axis starting at 19h29m00s and also because the available connection axis is on a 1 or 0 basis, i.e. connection available or unavailable.

Figure 25: Network availability graph from the 'ping_log' table.

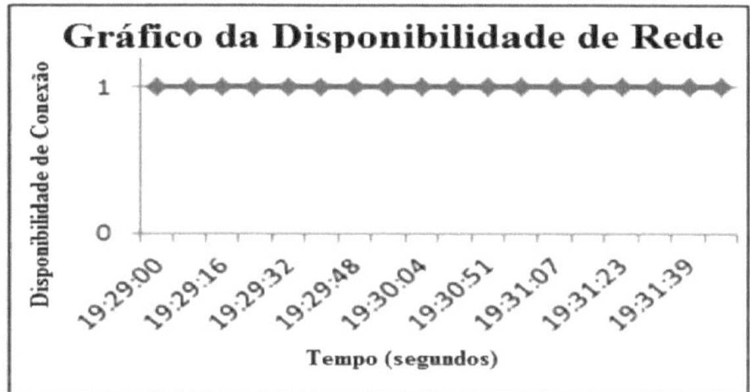

Source: Adapted and Reproduced from IP VIDEO DELIVERY COST: AN ANALYSIS...(OLIVEIRA *et al* ,2015 A)

It is crucial to note that these results go beyond a general assessment of network availability, allowing the same data analysis to be carried out separately or jointly, i.e. for each URL or for a set of resources. Therefore, the responsibility for availability is divisible by CDN provider, for example. However, if most or all of the URLs under verification start transmitting failed connection reports and if they are from different providers, such as those in the table above, it is reasonable to consider that the responsibility may lie with the Broadband Providers (ISPs).

Ultimately, behind a total availability register, there is the simultaneous creation of a charging mechanism for the end user that can only reduce the ISP or CDN's bill. Suppose a user sets the software to catalog network availability information for a month. And, once the month is over, it calculates the consumer's EMFNA result to be X%. In case, he pays $Y monthly for the service of a BP, he could claim to pay only an amount is equal to the multiplication of $Y times X%, as a way to get a compensation for the connection not being delivered or connection request not being reached for period of equivalent to the time he was offline. Imagine that X is 85%, Y is $100 and the month is 30 days long. The customer can either request a $15 ($100 - 85) discount, paying only $85 ($100 * 85%), or request a period of 4.5 days (30 days * 15%) free of connection charges. For a corporate client, one period could be more significant than another, such as business hours. In this contract, hours between 9 a.m. and 5 p.m. could have a weight of 75% while hours from 5 p.m. to 9 a.m. corresponded to a weight of 25% in the weighted average. And, this could certainly be reflected in the analysis captured through this software, since all the tests are automatically recorded with the date and time they took place.

In appreciation, since the current scenario of global computer networks presents a questionable service for the growing demands of consumers. And, as content continually migrates to IP, its inherent limitations tend to diminish connection availability. Consequently, ways of detecting these failures are essential, especially when monitoring needs to be distributed, continuous, support modifications over time, consume a minimum of hardware processing, require a low network throughput impact and run on different end-user devices.

The proposed methodology presents a viable solution to these challenges, producing a real-time evaluation of the network, associated with a customization strategy that is even manageable by the user during testing. Through this routine, the uplink-downlink interval delivered by a CDN or ISP is exhaustively examined. This allows customers to technically prove whether a resource was available or not, providing effective contract control over these paid services. This user-side billing is a key deliverable of this application, bringing financial advantages and protecting consumers from undersold QoS. It is imperative to remember that the application has been developed entirely on open source architectures, i.e. without any ownership costs.

Another point of this work is to reveal the difficult task of transferring services that are traditionally transmitted by TV systems to Web Stream. It exposes the fact that a packet-based network such as the Internet requires an excessive technical effort to take on the role of a traditional television system, especially when considering live events aimed at numerous viewers. The question therefore arises as to whether the significant investments needed to make live broadcasts on the web possible are worth it. But as this seems to be an unchangeable future, users need to be vigilant and demand that they are served as promised in their contracts. And if, eventually, they are not delivered in the correct way, they should claim their due refunds through technical measurement for a correct cost-effectiveness.

5.3. Software for Audience Capture Associated with Video Stream Availability

The operation of the extension installed in the browser for the user, the Front-end, as well as the display of the collections (captured data) for the user in the Back-end are described below.

5.3.1. Operation

For the application developed, the user first needs to access the 'Chrome Web Store - Extensions' or 'Chrome Extension Store' on the Internet via the Google Chrome browser. Once there, by searching for 'Youtube Data Stats', which is how this software was named, the icon and application described in Figure 26 will appear to be installed in the user's browser, available by accessing the address: 'https://chrome.google.com/webstore/detail/youtube-data-stats/nmnaacknlpckjpccicgekcno gaeoaipi'.

Figure 26: Page to install the Extension from the 'Chrome Web Store - Extensions'.

Source: Own figure

Clicking on the blue '+ USE IN CHROME' button displays a confirmation message to install and add the extension to the browser. This screen is shown in Figure 27 below and also informs the user that the application will have access to. These questions are standard and generated by Google itself after approving the application and making it available in the store, due to privacy policies.

Figure 27 Screen to confirm the installation of the browser extension with information on what the application will access from the user's browsing data.

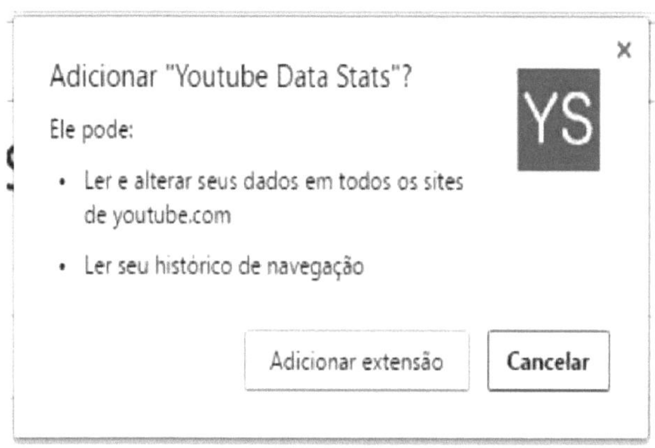

Source: Own figure

After the confirmation requested in Figure 27, clicking on 'Add Extension' displays the message shown in Figure 28. This shows where the application icon will be, located in the top right-hand corner of the browser. It also tells you how it will behave. In other words, it will be 'visible' by changing shades from black and white to color when it is not active on the current page. And assuming red and white, these colors and symbol have been programmed to be displayed like this, for when it is activated on the page the user is accessing.

Figure 28 Newsletter showing the confirmed installation of the Extension as well as the location of the icon indicating the active and inactive status of the application.

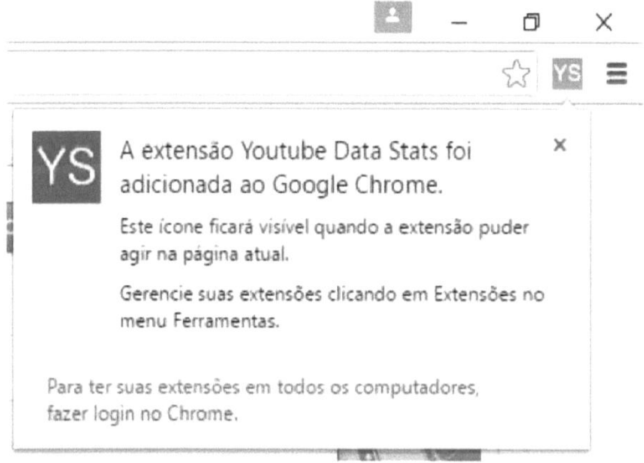

Source: Own figure

After installation, when the user accesses any audiovisual content on the site Youtube, the application will ask you to fill in the user's city, age and gender, through the sequential screens illustrated in Figures 29, 30 and 31 below. These three questions, as explained above, are asked until the user answers them, and are set up in a mandatory loop that demands an answer. These questions are only asked once, when the user accesses the first video after installing the software. It is worth noting that this information is saved locally in cookies, and is sent and repeated with each time audiovisual content is monitored.

Figure 29 Screen for users to fill in their city information.

Source: Own figure

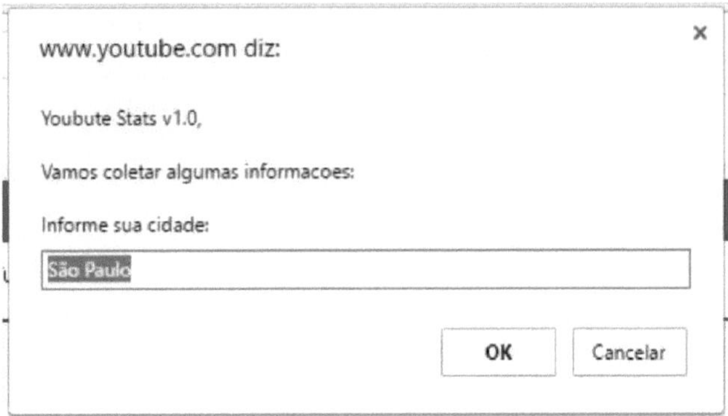

Figure 30 Screen for users to fill in their age.
Source: Own figure

Figure 31 Screen for users to fill in their gender information.
Source: Own figure

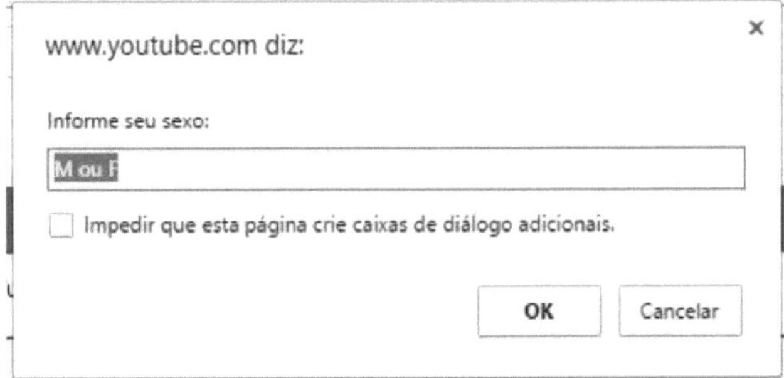

Next, in Figure 32, the application is active on the page while a video is being viewed by the user. At this point, it means that the codes previously described in the methodology chapter about this software are working to capture the information required in order to obtain information about the audience of this IP broadcast.

Figure 32: Example of the Active Extension running while a YouTube video is being accessed.
Source: Own figure

Figures 33 and 34 show, respectively, how the user is informed if the extension is active or inactive on the codes and APIs of the page it is accessing. This happens when a YouTube video is being searched for. Thus, in Figure 33, the colored extension icon means that the application is acting, its codes are interacting with those of the page. While in Figure 34, with the black and white icon, it is inactive, which occurs when the user is not accessing a YouTube video.

Figure 33: Extension icon indicating active application.

Source: Own figure

Figure 34 Extension icon indicating inactive application.

Source: Own figure

Another feature of the front-end software is shown in Figure 35, and is related to the aforementioned issues of monitoring which URL the user is accessing. This screen appears when the user performs an action to leave a video page and not go to another Youtube video. In other words, if they go from one video to another, this doesn't happen. Now, if he goes to a page that is not a YouTube video, if he closes the tab or the entire browser, this browser confirmation screen is displayed. And when he clicks the 'Leave this page' button, all the data collected on that page is sent to the centralizer after that click and if he stays on the page, monitoring continues normally. This confirmation page proved necessary in order to deactivate the application and not lose captured information.

Figure 35 Page exit confirmation screen - deactivates the application and sends information to the Back-end.

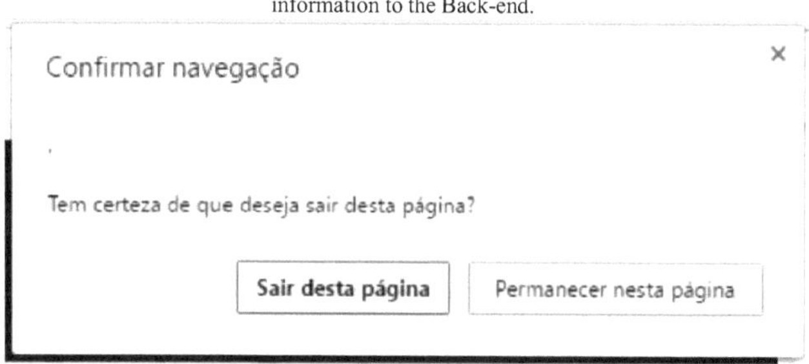

Source: Own figure

5.3.2 Captured data

The data captured from all the tests carried out by all the users is sent to the Back-end WebService, which is accessible via the interfaces described in the following figures. It should be noted that this data is available on the Internet and can be accessed by anyone with access to the system. Figure 36 shows the home page, which is a login screen, set up like this for security reasons, requesting an ID and password.

Figure 36: Software back-end login screen.

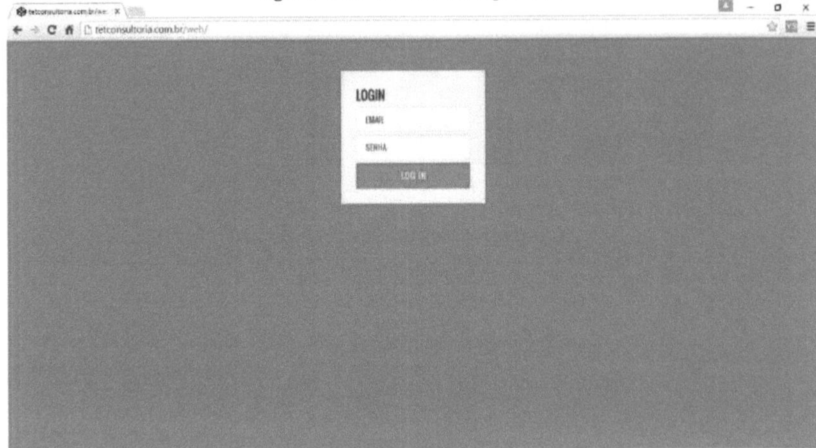

Source: Own figure

Figure 37 shows the page after a login authorized by the system. The logged-in user has the option of clicking on 'Search' to display everything in the database configured to store the collection information. 'Search' makes the selection in the database for the search to be displayed just below the word 'LIST', as this is where the selection is configured to be displayed.

Figure 37: Screen for entering and searching the data captured in the software's back-end.

Source: Own figure

Figure 38 shows the page after clicking on 'Search'. It shows the result of the search in the database, displaying all the data captured in the form of a table that follows the sequence from the most recent to the oldest information sent to the centralizer.

Figure 38: Search result screen displaying data captured in the software's back-end.

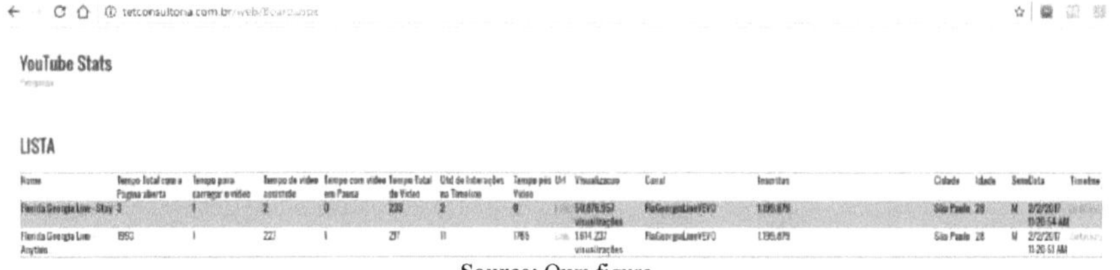

Source: Own figure

In order to detail this display of the search carried out, Figure 39 shows all the data captured from two tests sent to the Back-end. From left to right we have the columns with the information Name, Time Watched, Total Time, URL, Viewing, Channel, Subscribers, City, Age, Gender, Date.

Figure 39 Details of some of the results of the database search with the data captured in the software's back-end.

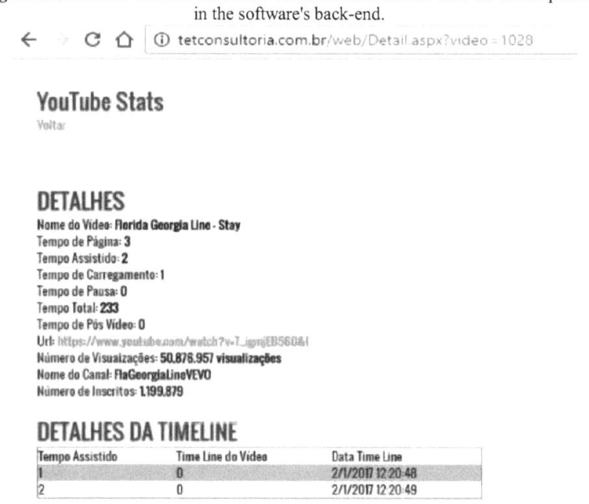

Source: Own figure

With regard to the data captured, it is important to note that, for the purposes of the audience, the most sensitive data and the data that generates the evaluation are the time values collected. In other words, the Total Time of the video and the Time Watched. This is because if, for example, you divide one by the other, you already have an interesting piece of data, which would inform you of the audience percentage for a given video. And with the other data we could relate this to views by date/time, by audience, by channel and, of course, by specific content. In the examples detailed in Figure 38, we would have 92s divided by 325s and 4s divided by 325s (seconds). This would give us 28.3% and 1.2% of the audience for that viewer of that content at that time. In addition, concerns about quality can also be seen, albeit partially, in this data. Since, as a subjective matter, if the content is of acceptable quality the user will watch it for longer, if it is not acceptable to them, they will not watch it.

5.3.2.1 Analysis of the Data Captured to Benchmark

Availability

To delve deeper into the question of availability, i.e. how to know if something is available as soon as it is demanded, i.e. latency, the first piece of data we have is the time it takes to load the Video. The following metrics figures show how the data looks with 1281 samples, divided into the metrics figures described below.

In Figure 40, referring to the Time to Load the General Video, we have the arithmetic mean line representing the value of 3.59s and the initial latency values. That is, the time for the content to start being displayed out of 1281 samples. Of these, 6.32% are equal to or longer than 10 seconds, 0.54% are 9s, 0.54% are 8s, 0.70% are 7s, 1.09% are 6s, 0.54% are 5s, 1.24% are 4s, 1.79% are 3s, 9.85% are 2s, 48.10% are 1s and 29.29% are 0s. This means that 87.24% are within 2 seconds. In addition to the average of 3.59s, dispersion calculations were carried out, obtaining a value of 24.83s for the standard deviation and 616.46s^2 for the variance. Observing the concentration of values, weighted mean and standard deviation calculations were carried out, but the values obtained did not change significantly. Thus, an analysis excluding samples greater than or equal to 10 seconds, or 6.32% of the data, shows an average of 1.09s, a standard deviation of 1.39s and a variance of 1.96s^2 There is a significant variation in the time taken to load the videos, with different buffering times, with a tendency towards stochastic and increasing variation for data organized over time.

Figure 40 Time to load General Video.

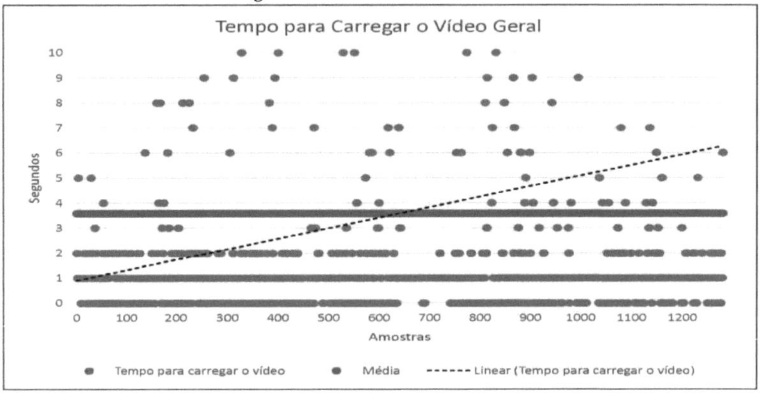

Source: Own figure

Chart Fact Sheet:
Standard Deviation: 24.83sVariance : 616.46s^2 Average: 3.59s
06.32% >10s 00.54% 9s00. 54% 8s 00.70% 7s01. 09% 6s00. 54% 5s
01.24% 4s 01.79% 3s 09.85% 2s 48.10% 1s29 .29% 0s
87.24% up to 2s
No significant changes with weighted mean and standard deviation calculations.
Excluding samples >10 (06.32%)
Standard Deviation: 1.39s Variance: 1.96s^2 Mean: 1.09s
Features:
Significant Variation in Time to Load Videos;
Different buffering times;
Trend of stochastic and increasing variation (for data organized over time).
Note: This refers to initial latency.

Figure 41 shows the Time to Load Broadband Video graph, i.e. the initial latency display for broadband network connections and notebook accesses. Here you can see the distribution of the data, as well as a comparison with the arithmetic mean of 5.01 seconds. In addition, dispersion calculations were carried out to obtain a standard deviation of 32.85 seconds and a variance of 1078.812. It can also be seen that the tests showed low variation, uniform buffering, high stability with a tendency to grow slightly. Despite the higher values than the previous graph with the general values, the convergence to stability was significant.

Figure 41 Time to Load Broadband Video.

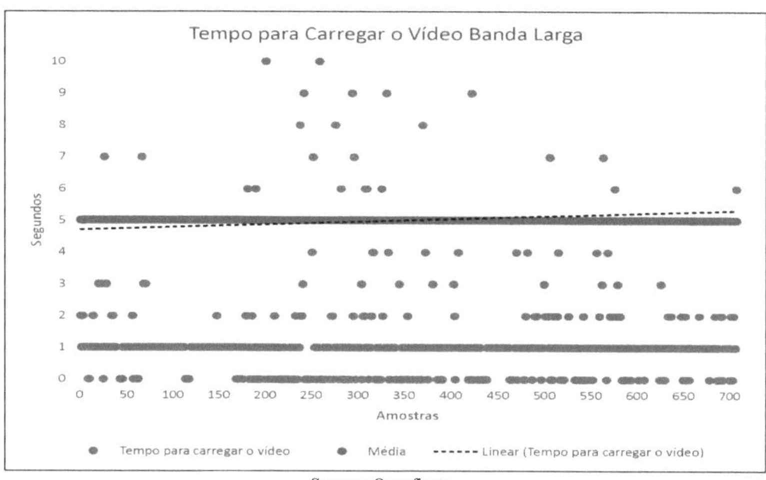

Source: Own figure

Chart Fact Sheet:
Standard Deviation: 32.85s Variance: 1078.81s^2 Average: 5.01s
Features:
Low variation in video loading times;
Uniform initial buffering;
High stability.

Figure 42 shows the Video Load Time for Mobile Network connections with Static Equipment. This is relative to the tests with Mobile Networks through a *Smartphone* mobile device routing its mobile Internet connection over Wi-Fi to the Notebook with both static equipment within a built environment in an urban area. It is worth noting that the arithmetic mean was 4.68 seconds, which was lower than the initial latency for broadband access. However, it showed high variability, as well as a significant downward trend in initial buffering time and low stability. Computations to observe the distribution of values showed a standard deviation of 13.19s and a variance of 174.10s^2 .

Figure 42 Time to Load Video on Mobile Network Connection with Equipment Static.

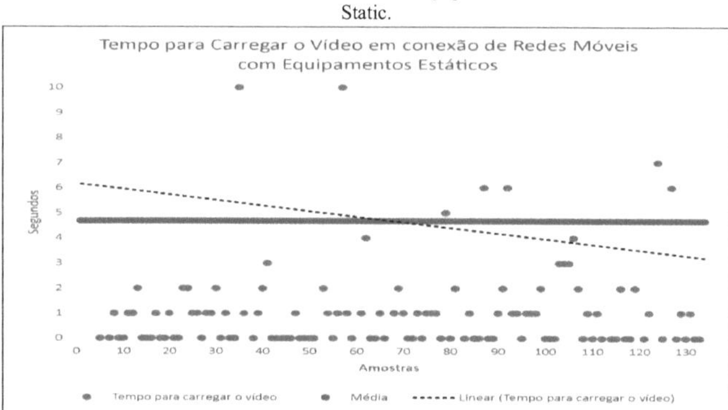

Source: Own figure

Chart Fact Sheet:
Standard Deviation: 13.19s Variance: 174.10s^2
Features:
High Variation in Time to Load Videos;

Initial decreasing buffering;
Low stability.
Average: 4.68s

Figure 43 shows the graph entitled Time to Load Video on Mobile Network Connections with Equipment in Motion. This, like the previous one, shows samples of experiments with Mobile Networks using a *Smartphone* handset routing its mobile Wi-Fi Internet connection to the Notebook. However, in this case, both the cell phone and the notebook were in motion inside a motor vehicle traveling through a metropolitan area. This resulted in an arithmetic average of 1.32 seconds, one of the lowest overall averages observed in these analyses. And, following this arrangement, the dispersion values obtained mathematically showed a standard deviation of 3.49s and a variance of 12.212. It is worth drawing the interpretation that there was little variation in the initial loading time of the content, uniform initial buffering and a high level of stability.

Figure 43 Time to Load Video on Mobile Network Connections with Equipment in Motion.

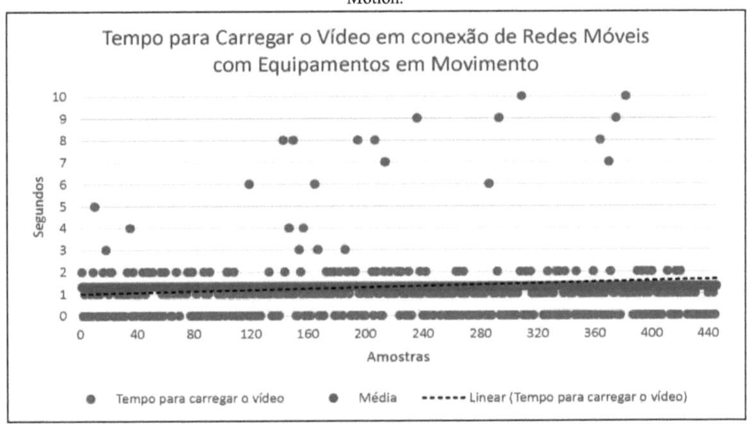

Source: Own figure

Chart Fact Sheet:
Standard Deviation: 3.49s Variance: $12.21s^2$
Features:
Low Variation in Time to Load Videos;
Uniform Initial Buffering;
High stability.
Average: 1.32s

Figure 44 shows the graph of the experiment called No automatic playlist, No user registered with Google, With IP and location masking via VPN (*Virtual Private Network*). It should be noted that these tests were conducted with a broadband connection. The main objective was to demonstrate the impact when the user wishes to be anonymous, using robust privacy mechanisms such as those provided by a Virtual Private Network (VPN). This case study presented the highest arithmetic mean value of 7.31 seconds and the dispersion calculations followed this increase, with a standard deviation of 57.03s and a variance of 3252.40s 2. While, for results organized over time, the upward trend is expressive. In addition, it is characterized by high variation in the initial video loading time, increasing initial latency buffering and low stability.

Figure 44: Time to load the Video with Anonymous Browsing - No Automatic Playlist, No Google Registered User, With IP and location masking via VPN.

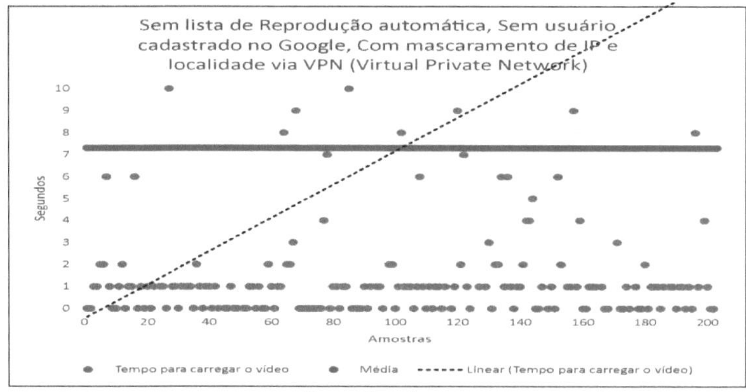

Source: Own figure

High Variation in Time to Load Videos;
Increasing initial buffeting;
Low stability.

Figure 45 shows the graph entitled With automatic playlist, Without user registered with Google, With IP and location masking via VPN (*Virtual Private Network*). In these tests, we observed an evolution in relation to the study carried out in Figure 44. This is because Figure 45 shows the user's discovery, i.e. the partial loss of privacy over time, i.e. a reduction in the effects of the masking provided by the VPN. Therefore, the average of these experiments was 2.85 seconds and the distribution was calculated as 7.81s standard deviation and 60.96s variance^2 . This also translates into low variation in the initial audiovisual loading time, uniform buffering in terms of initial latency and high stability. The general linear trend, although significantly uniform and stable, shows a slight upward trend over time. This led to a better result in terms of availability, with a reduction in the loading time.

Figure 45: Time to Load Video with Incognito Browsing - With Automatic Playlist , Without User Registered with Google, With IP and Location Masking via VPN.

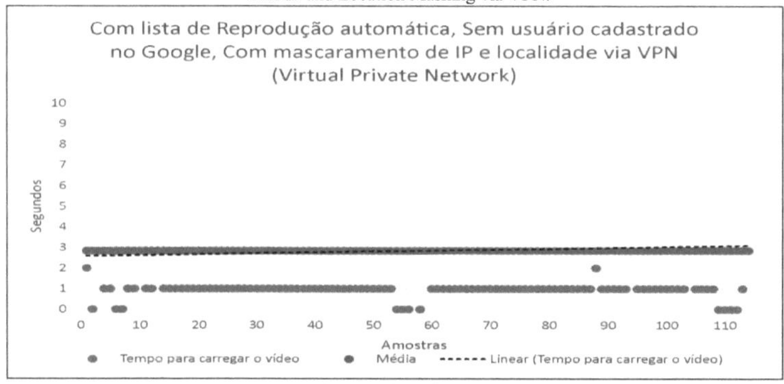

Source: Own figure

Chart Fact Sheet:
Standard Deviation: 57.03sVariance : 3252.40s^2 Average: 7.31s
Features:
Chart Fact Sheet:
Standard Deviation: 7.81sVariance : 60.96s2 Mean: 2.85s
Features:
Low Variation in Time to Load Videos;
Uniform Initial Buffering; High Stability.

Continuing with the question of availability, the relationship between the time the video is paused, a figure that includes the sum of user and system pauses and crashes, and the number of interactions on the *timeline*. Figure 47, Time with Paused Video X Number of Interactions on the *Timeline,* shows the relationship. In this analysis, the tests showed a dependency: the greater the number of interactions with the content, the longer the time the content is paused. In other words, the more unavailable the audiovisual, the more crashes and consequently the poorer the user experience. The number of interactions indicates all the times the video was interacted with, either by user or by system. And it should be noted that this value is considerably increased the more times the frames are loaded in the episodes in which the user and/or the system clicks and/or moves over the video time bar. In addition, the value increases proportionally in relation to the number of frames loaded by the system, as exemplified by Figure 46.

Analysis of the video pause time data shows that 53.32% of the tests had 0 seconds, 21.08% had 1s, 0.86% had 2s, 1.56% had 3s, 1.95% had 4s, 1.80% had 5s, 1.87% had 6s, 0.94% had 7s, 1.09% had 8s, 1.17% had 9s and 14.36% had values equal to or greater than 10 seconds. There is a cluster of 74.40% of the tests conducted with a value of up to 1 second. While the arithmetic mean was 78.02s and the data dispersion calculations gave a standard deviation of 949.62s and a variance of 901.778.15s^2 The weighted mean and weighted standard deviation were also calculated and did not show any significant changes. In this way, the same cut was made as previously observed, in order to extract more information from the data captured. In other words, in order to observe the behavior of the data concentration, excluding samples greater than or equal to 10s, an average of 0.95s, a standard deviation of 1.92s and a variance of 3.69s were obtained^2 .

When studying the number of interactions, it can be seen that 2.97% have 1 interaction, 4.29% have 2 interactions, 29.12% have 3 interactions, 13.19% have 4 interactions, 26.23% have 5 interactions, 6.01% have 6 interactions, 2.11% have 7 interactions, 1.87% have 8 interactions, 1.64% have 9 interactions and 12.57% have 10 or more interactions. It also appears that 75.80% of the samples have up to 5 interactions. By calculating the layout and distribution of this data, we have an average of 18.08 interactions, a standard deviation of 86.56 interactions and a variance of 7,492.75 interactions^2 . Weighted computations such as the weighted mean and weighted standard deviation were also carried out, which did not show any significant changes. In order to gather information on the concentration of the data, values with 10 or more interactions were removed and the arithmetic mean was 4.16 interactions, the standard deviation was 1.55 interactions and the variance was 2.42 interactions^2 .

Furthermore, there is a measure of dependence between these two types of data, with a positive correlation and a coefficient of 0.06. Although this value is low, it tends to increase the more trials are considered in the calculation. Furthermore, it can be seen that when a margin of 5% is taken into account in the values of pause time or interactions, more or less, the coefficient tends to show an index referring to a perfect correlation, denoting a high measure of dependence.

Figure 46: Number of Interactions on the YouTube Video Timeline via uploaded Frames.

Source: Reproduced and Adapted from For the Love of Physics (Walter Lewin's Last Lecture). (Lewin, 2014)

For the Love of Physics (Walter Lewin's Last Lecture)

Figure 47: Time with Video in Pause X Number of Interactions on Timeline.

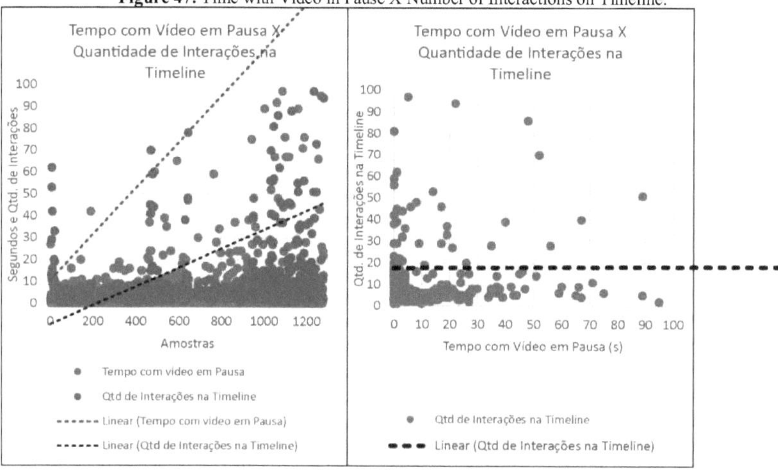

Source: Own figure

Information Sheet for Time with Video Pause:

Standard Deviation: 949.62s Variance: 901,778.15s^2 Average: 78.02s

14.36% >10s01. 17% 9s01. 09% 8s00 .94% 7s01. 87% 6s01. 80% 5s 01.95% 4s01. 56% 3s00 .86% 2s <u>21.08% 1s53. 32% 0s</u>

<u>74.40% up to 1s</u>

No significant changes with weighted calculations of mean and standard deviation. Excluding samples >10 (14.36%)

Standard Deviation: 1.92sVariance : 3.69s^2 Average: 0.95s

Information Sheet for Number of Interactions(i) on *Timeline* :

Standard Deviation: 86.56sVariance : 7,492.75s^2 Average: 18.08s

12.57% >10i 01.64% 9i01. 87% 8i 02.11% 7i06 .01% 6i <u>26.23% 5i</u> <u>13.19% 4i 29.12% 3i04 .29% 2i 2.97% 1i</u>

<u>75.80% up to 5i</u>

No significant changes with weighted mean and standard deviation calculations.

Excluding samples >10 (12.57%)

Standard Deviation: 1.55i Variance: 2.42i^2 Mean: 4.16i

Features:

Relationship: The More Interactions, the Longer the Pause Time. Therefore, more unavailable content, more crashes and impoverishment of the user experience. Positive correlation between Pause and Interactions with a coefficient of 0.06 which, with a margin of +-5%, tends towards perfect correlation.

Note 1: Video Pause Time includes both user and system pauses.

Note 2: Number of Interactions indicates all the times the user and/or system interacted with the Video.

The analysis in Figures 48 and 49 below shows a comparison between the time taken to load the video and its relationship with the time after the video. They show that the initial latency time varies with and without automatic playback. Since the time to load the next content is shorter when the autoplay option is selected, the video is preloaded. Remember that these are the same tests for which the conditions were clarified when looking at the metrics in Figures 44 and 45, respectively.

When analyzing Figure 48, referring to Time to Load Video X Time after Video (VPN without Auth. Rep.), we see a significant marriage of these two variables. However, the time after the video does not influence the initial audiovisual latency period and vice versa. This is because we didn't find a relationship that could be considered significantly beneficial, but detrimental. This relationship shows that even with high times after the videos, the upward trend is replicated for the loading time at the beginning of the videos. It is evident that the adoption of total privacy provided through the Virtual Private Network in a schematic without the use of Automatic Playback, avoided the possible provisioning for pre-loading and transmission alignment. Therefore, the value of the post-video time, whether low or high, did not positively influence the tendency for the initial latency to increase over the test period. It is worth noting that this behavior is due to the randomness with which the videos were chosen, so the time after the video was not used to load the next content. In addition, calculations were carried out on the measure of dependence between the data sets for each time and a positive and high correlation coefficient was obtained, which gives a correlation close to perfect with a value of 0.96.

Figure 48: Time to Load Video vs. Time After Video (VPN without Autorep).

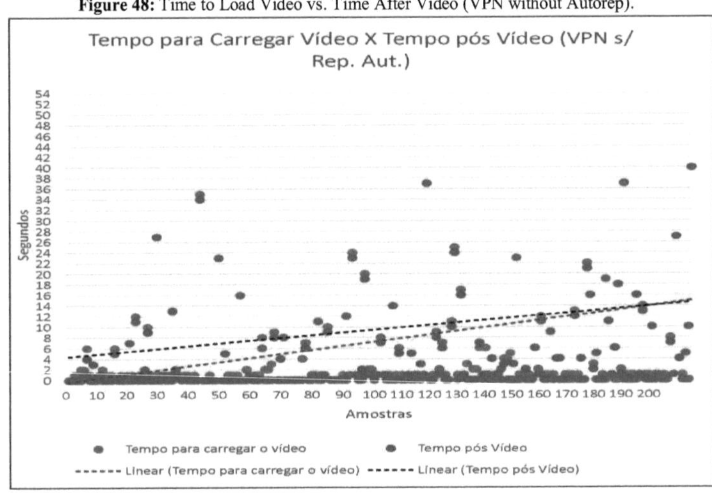

Source: **Own figure**

Chart Fact Sheet:

Features:

Times have no effect on each other;

No relevant relationship;

Positive correlation between Initial Latency Time and Post-Video Time with a coefficient of 0.96, close to perfect correlation;

As the next videos are chosen at random, the Post Video Time is not used to load the next one.

In Figure 49 Time to Load Video X Time After Video (VPN w/ Rep. Aut.), we can see the relevance of the aforementioned partial loss of privacy or discovery of the user by the system. This is evidenced by the significant relationship between the two variables denoting time, which indicates that both the activation and consequent follow-up of Autoplay together with Post-Video Time act to reduce the initial Video Load Time. This reduction contributes to the high stability and uniformity of the loading times observed. Likewise, it is clearer that the reduction in privacy helps to ensure that the transmission has better levels of availability. Furthermore, the correlation obtained is close to perfect with a value of 0.91, the difference being that in this case it acted beneficially by helping to reduce the loading time.

Figure 49 : Time to Load Video vs. Time After Video (VPN w/ Autorep).

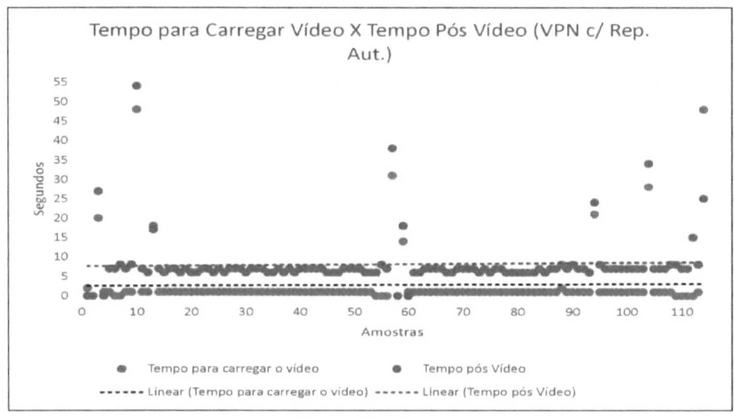

Source: Own figure

Chart Fact Sheet:
Features:
Positive correlation between Initial Latency Time and Post-Video Time with a coefficient of 0.91, close to perfect correlation;
Times with meaningful relationships;
Post-video time reduces loading time;
Stability and uniformity of timings.
Note: The points outside the trend show video crashes. In these, you can see that the content initially loads and the next video loads.

Staying on the subject of availability, Figures 50 and 51 compare the number of subscribers to the channel and the number of views against the initial latency of the video, i.e. the time it takes to load the page. This shows the influence that these two indicators can have on availability.

Figure 50 shows the graphical format of Number of Views X Time to Load Video. The number of times the content has been watched has a beneficial effect on reducing loading time. The more views an audiovisual has, the less time it will take to start playing. It can be seen that videos with 200 million views or more have a loading time of 0.9 seconds. In addition, videos with an equal or greater number of views tend to be within 0 to 2 seconds of initial loading latency. It should be remembered that 29.29% of the tests had 0s, 48.10% had 1s and 09.85% had 2 seconds.

Figure 50 Number of Views X Time to Load Video.

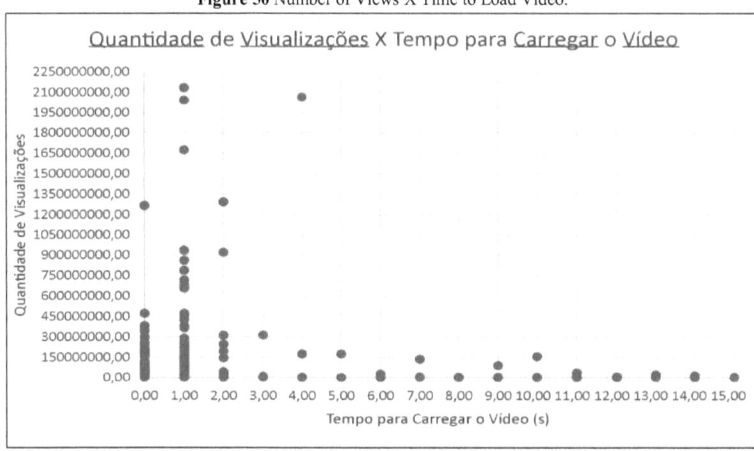

Source: Own figure

While Figure 51 shows the Number of Subscribers X Time to Load Video. In this context, the number of subscribers showed a significant influence from 2.5 million with values for initial latency time concentrated at 1.0 seconds. It also significantly established the tendency for the data sets to be proportionally inverted in some way. That is, in the sense that when the number of users subscribed to a given channel increases, the initial loading time tends to be shorter, being in the range of up to 2 seconds. It's important to remember that 87.24% of the tests were up to 2s.

In addition to the above, it can be seen that the influence of both the number of views and the number of subscribers is relative, being strongly linked to a "trending" status. A "trending" piece of content and/or channel is one that has seen an increase in the aforementioned quantities over a short period of time, usually within a week. The more current this "up" is, the greater the influence of these quantities, i.e. the effect is greater when a recent crescendo is identified, which classifies the audiovisual and/or channel as "up".

Figure 51 : Number of Subscribers X Time to Load Video.

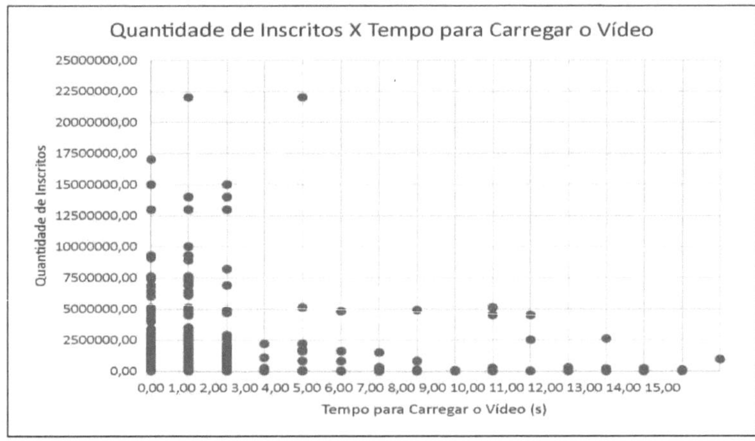

Source: Own figure

Information sheet for Metric Figures 50 and 51:

<u>09.85% 2s 48.10% 1s 29.29% 0s</u>

<u>87.24% up to 2s.</u>

Features:

Influence is relative: If the content is "on the rise", with a recent increase in views/subscribers, the tendency is for the content to be available;

Both have a positive and relatively inversely proportional influence on initial latency availability; Views: from 0.2 billion there were times concentrated in 0.9s (approx.); Subscribers: from 2.5 million there were times concentrated in 1.0s (approx.); Number of views shows greater influence if average loading times are considered.

Number of subscribers denotes a greater influence on availability, considering the absolute values;

Still on the subject of availability, the following comparisons are interesting to fully understand. In Figure 52 below, we have the Total Time with the Page Open and the Total Video Time. In this figure, although we don't yet have the value of time watched, we can already get a glimpse of the audience, noting that the less time on the page, the less chance there is of a high audience, in terms of time viewed. In this analysis we see a high abandonment rate, but lower than the rate reported by the provider, of 90% evasion up to 10 seconds, with around 30.68% of users staying up to 10 seconds. The Total Time of the videos follows the trend reported by the provider in question, with 59.09% of the videos lasting up to 300 seconds, or 5 minutes. In the Metrics Figure analyzed, it should be noted that the marriage in the middle of the graph in the values above the sample number 600 and below the sample number 800. In other words, the near-equality of the times is marked for the autoplay experiments, when the videos were viewed in their entirety. It can also be seen that the concentration of the Total Time with the Page Open is 210s, or 3.5 minutes, which is the average of these times. And, considering a margin of 1 minute, more or less in this time, there are 49.09% of the videos that were shown, excluding those that showed a gap of up to 10 seconds, for videos up to and including 299 seconds (YouTube, 2017).

Figure 52 Total Time with Page Open X Total Video Time.

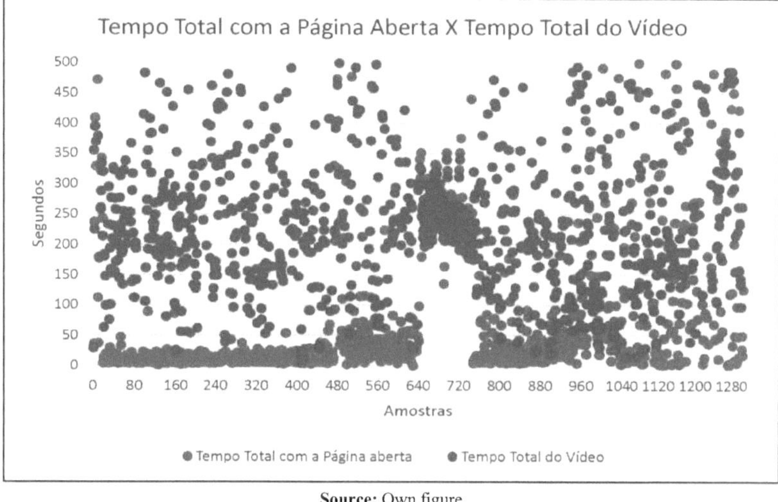

Source: Own figure

Chart Fact Sheet:
Average Total Time with Page Open without the values that evaded by up to 10s, for videos up to and including 299s: 210s.
Features:
Concentrated Total Time with Page Open between 150s and 270s, inclusive. 210s with a 60s margin.
Abandonment rate: 30.68% abandon the page within 10 seconds. Provider: 90%.
Total time of videos viewed follows the trend reported by the provider: 59.09% are up to 300s;
The merging occurred significantly during the autoplay tests, when the videos were watched in their entirety;
Note: The audience is visible.

Figure 53 refers to the Total Time with the Page Open minus the Video Watched Time compared to the Post-Video Time. This provides an insight into how long the content required by the user took, i.e. it was more likely to be unavailable for delivery. This is because since the Post-Video Time is low in comparison, as can be seen below, this total time with the page open subtracted from the time watched gives us how long the user waited for the content without receiving it, as well as how this varies from sample to sample. Furthermore, it can be seen that the Total Time with Page Open minus the Video Watched Time value corresponds to the Post-Video Time. It shows a positive correlation of 0.16. This value, although low, indicates a behavior. Therefore, with a margin of 5%, more or less of one set or the other, it offers a tendency towards a perfect coefficient for measuring dependence. This correspondence collaborates with the discovery of the Post-Video Time, which is a relevant factor for availability in cases such as automatic playback and the provision of suggested videos on the side, a selection which, as we observed, if followed, brings benefits for availability. This mathematical operation allows the time data to be obtained after the video and vice versa. In this way, it provides the data even without collecting it and is used to check for errors, as well as to check the consistency of the values captured.

Figure 53 Total Time with Page Open minus Video Time Watched X Post Time Video.

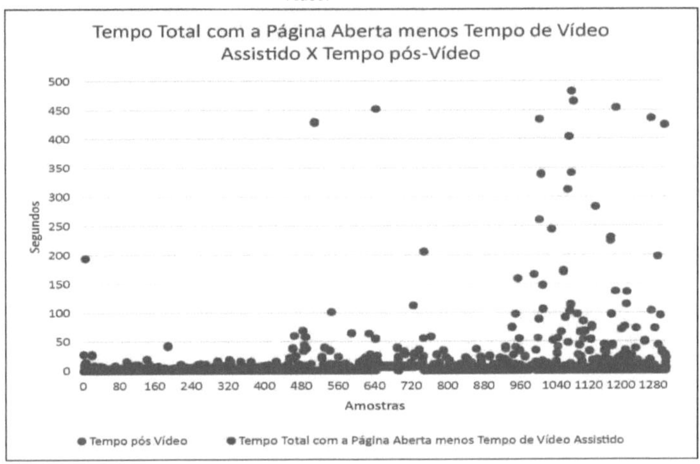

Chart Fact Sheet:
Features:
Total Open Page Time minus Watched Video Time = Post-Video Time Positive correlation between 'Total Open Page Time minus Watched Video Time' and 'Post-Video Time' with a coefficient of 0.16 which, with a margin of +-5%, tends towards perfect correlation;
This correspondence collaborates with the discovery of the Post-Video Time, which is a relevant factor for availability for cases such as selected autoplay followed by efficient video delivery;
Subtraction provides the possibility of obtaining the data even without collecting it, or if there is an error, as well as checking the consistency of captured values.

Continuing with the question of how available the IP Stream content is, Figure 54 compares the Total Time with the Page Open, the Video Watched Time and the Video Paused Time. This graph shows the relationship between the times in order to gain an understanding of availability. The video pause time is the sum of all user and system interruptions and interruptions after the start of the broadcast. The graph shows how these times vary and how long the user waits for the content, i.e. the duration of the unavailability. It can be seen that the content had a variable latency to the point where it was perceived by the user. This is because the pause time includes intermittent crashes, episodes in which the page was left loading, whether caused by the system and/or the user. The trends in pause times can be seen in ascending order from shortest to longest: VPN Autoplay, data located in the center of the graph from test number 600 and before 800; Broadband, located on the far left from 0 to less than 450; VPN No Autoplay, located to the left of the center between more than 450 and less than 600;
Static Equipment Mobile Networks, to the right of center from sample number 800 and below 940; Moving Equipment Mobile Networks to the far right from 940 onwards. In addition, the dependency measures between page open times and time viewed showed a reasonable positive correlation coefficient of 0.51. The proportional gap in this value tends to equal the time paused, i.e. the difference between the period with the page open and the time watched tends to result in the time paused, a positive correlation close to perfect at 0.88.

Figure 54 Total Time with Page Open X Time Video Watched X Time Video Paused.

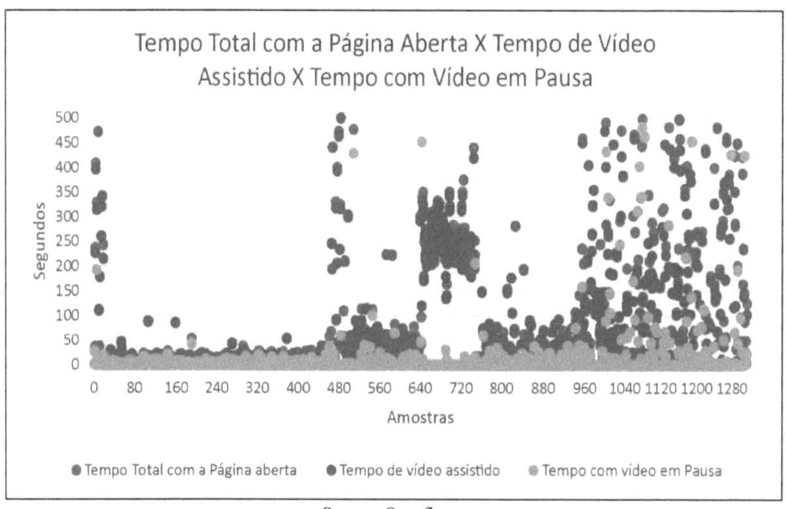

Source: Own figure

Chart Fact Sheet:
Positive correlation between Total Time Opened and Video Watched with a coefficient of 0.51.
Time with Page Open minus Time Video Watched and Time Video Paused have a close to perfect positive correlation of 0.88. The values are expressively close, indicating a high tendency for the content to remain paused.
Features:
Latency duration significantly variable to the point of being perceived by the user.
Time in Pause, in green, is the sum of system and user crashes.
Pause time in ascending order, from the shortest pause time to the longest:
VPN AutoPlay (center of graph) < | Availability Good (Best);
Broadband (left) < | Availability Reasonable;
VPN No AutoPlay (left of center) < | Low Availability;
Mobile Networks Static Equipment (right of center) < Poor Availability;
Mobile Networks Equipment in Motion (right) < | Availability Poor (Worst).

5.3.2.2 Analysis of the Data Captured to Measure Audience

In order to delve deeper into the audience issue, it is first necessary to carry out primary analysis to check the total percentage of all videos with their total size.

As a result, from the samples, the content had a 31.54% audience, as shown below in Figure 55, which shows the sum of all the video times watched divided by the total time of the video and gives us the individualized audience of each overall video as a percentage. It should be remembered that 90% of the videos viewed on YouTube have no more than 10 seconds of retention, and since the average length of videos is between 4 and 5 minutes, we can combine these various sources into 270 seconds. Thus, the audience of 90% of the videos would be up to 0.037 or 3.70%. We can also estimate the provider's overall average audience to be up to 13.33%, if we consider the remaining 10% to have a 100% audience. Therefore, comparisons and analyses show that user retention is higher than that reported by the provider, but with a certain relationship. This is because 35.25% of the total time actually watched is up to 10 seconds. And 40.11% watch up to 4% of the content. 57.41% watch up to 10% of the content, while 27.92% watch 50% or more of the video (Statistic Brain, 2016; YouTube, 2017).

Figure 55: General Audience.

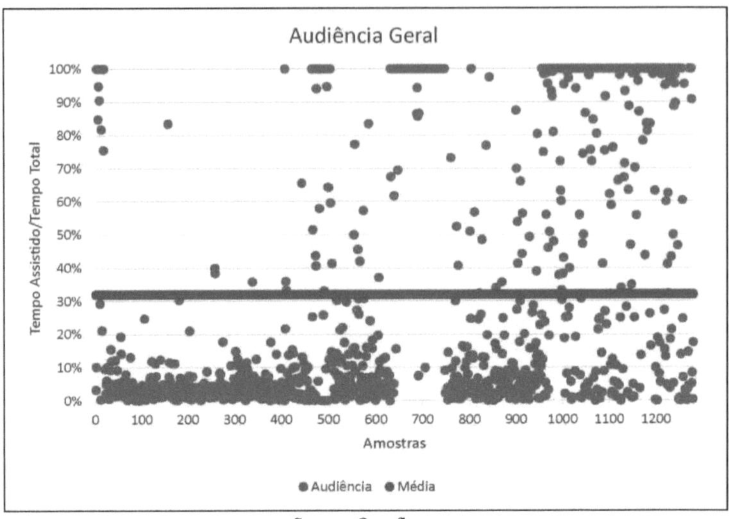

Source: Own figure

Graph Fact Sheet:
Features:
User retention proved to be higher than that reported by the provider, although with a certain relationship, as the levels of abandonment were significant;
The provider's overall average audience can be estimated at up to 13.33% by weighted average and the figure obtained was 31.54%;
For 35.25% there is evasion within 10 seconds;
With 40.11% you get views in up to 4% of the total video length;
And 57.41% watch up to 10% of the content;
While 27.92% watch at least 50% of the total length of the audiovisual accessed.
Note: It was found that this audience was not altered by the autoplay tests, as the other VPN tests neutralized this possible increase.

Continuing on the subject of audience, Figure 56 shows the effects of the number of subscribers the channel that published the video has. This diagram shows that the number of subscribers has an influence in the sense that the higher the number, the greater the audience. In other words, the trend shown is one of relatively proportional growth. The calculation of the measure of dependence between the observed data sets showed a positive correlation coefficient of 0.13, thus showing a beneficial but low dependence. These results follow an identical justification presented in the question of the availability of the enrolment value effects. In other words, the effect observed by the relationship manifests itself clearly when the content is classified as "up", with the aforementioned recent increase. Looking at the graph, as well as the breakdown of the samples, it can be seen that the content on the left, despite having a high number of subscribers, did not gain an audience. The result of the study shows that this content is generally old, published months and/or years ago, and was not classified as "on the rise". On the other hand, the results on the right, especially from 60% of the audience and 1.5 million subscribers onwards, are typified by being recent, published up to days and/or weeks ago, and/or also by having a greater number of "up" videos, whether new or not.

Figure 56 Number of subscribers vs. audience.

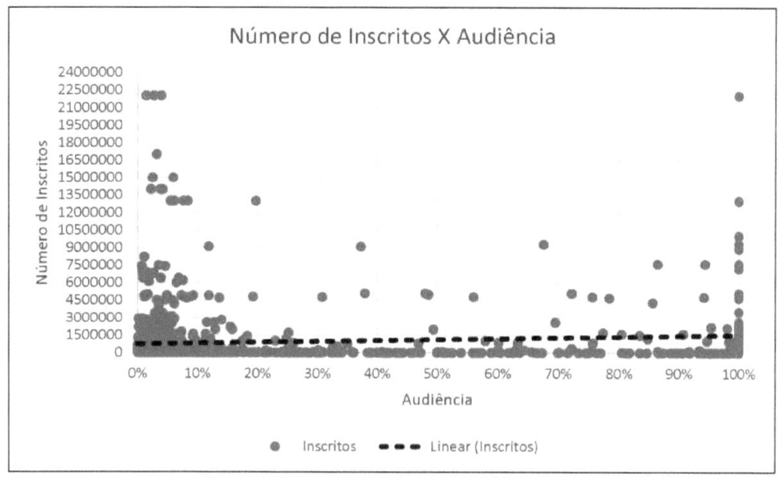

Source: Own figure

Figure 57 shows the influence of the number of views an audiovisual has on the audience. Similarly to the number of subscribers, the number of views has a favorable effect on audience growth. The dependency calculations show a positive correlation coefficient of 0.07 which, although classified as weak, indicates that the effect exists. However, as in the case of the number of subscribers, the influence is relative, depending not only on high values, but also on whether the content is recently increasing in views, or even "on the rise". The graph in Figure 57 shows a trend whereby the greater the number of views, the greater the audience. However, this effect proves to be significant in the tests with an 85% audience and 0.3 billion views, which also show the presence of content classified as "on the rise".

Figure 57 Views X Audience.

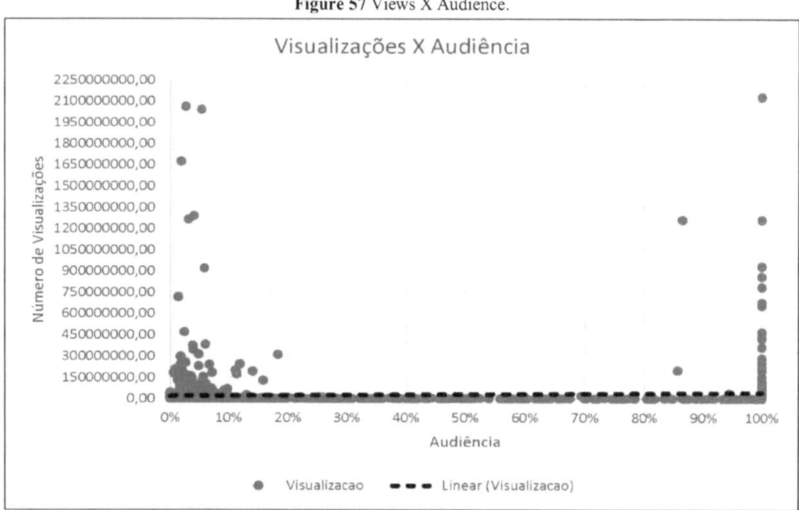

Source: Own figure

Information sheet for Metric Figures 56 and 57:

Features:

Influence is relative: If the content is "on the rise", with a recent increase in views/subscribers, the tendency is for the content to have high audience levels;

Both have a positive and relatively directly proportional influence on the audience;
Subscribers: significant effects from 60% audience and 1.5 million subscribers (approx.), positive correlation coefficient of 0.13;

Views: from 85% of the audience and 0.3 billion views (approx.) there is a significant trend, with a positive correlation coefficient of 0.07;
The number of subscribers has a greater influence on availability, considering the absolute values;
Number of views shows greater influence when considering average loading times.

Staying on the subject of factors that can have an impact on the audience, Figure 58 considers the Total Time with the Page Open. This analysis clearly shows that the more time invested in open content, the slightly greater the chance of a high audience rate. This characteristic is robustly expressed as can be seen in the trend line in the graph. However, it should be noted that the increase in audience is not proportional and/or direct, as this time value, when high, can also indicate poor broadcast quality, which affects audience negatively.

Figure 58 Total time the page is open X audience.

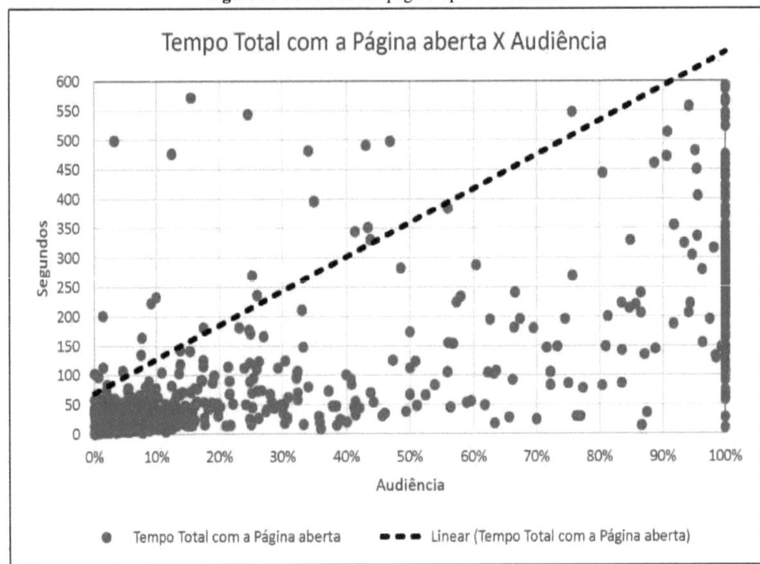

Source: Own figure

Chart Fact Sheet:
Features:
The longer the total time the page is open, the greater the tendency for the audience to rise, but without a significant relationship;
Low rapport, because a high time can also signal unsatisfactory quality, a factor that reduces the audience;
Growth trend, but weak.

In order to analyze the influence of interactions on the audience issue, Figure 59 was compiled to see the Number of Interactions on the Timeline vs. Audience. In this sense, it should be noted that if the amount of interactions increases, there is a weak tendency for the audience to grow, since this is one of the indicators of an impoverished user experience.

Figure 59: Number of Timeline Interactions X Audience.

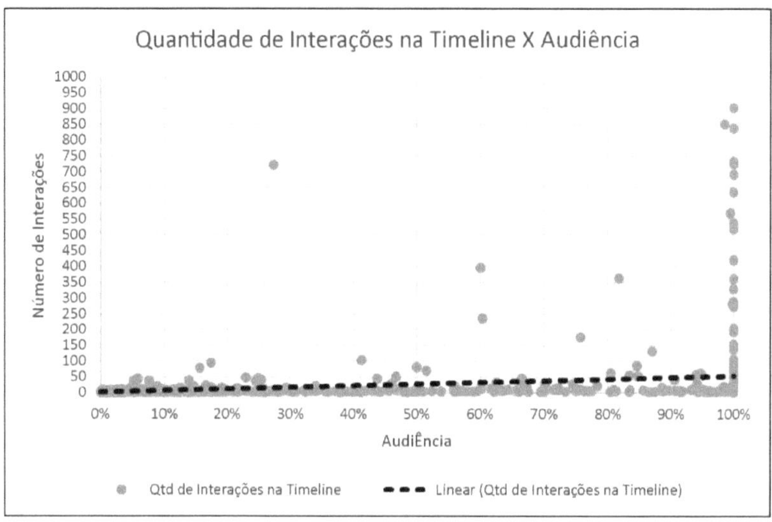

Source: Own figure

Chart Fact Sheet:
Features:
The greater the number of interactions on the timeline, the smaller the increase in the audience trend;
A high number of interactions is indicative of deteriorating quality;
Growing trend, but negligible.

And in Figure 60, the time taken to load the content showed no relevant effect. With this, it can be seen that unavailability causes a decline in the audience. However, the results show that users can wait to watch the content they want, but if this content takes a long time to load, their intention to watch it in full will be reduced.

Figure 60 Time to load video X Audience.

Tempo para carregar o vídeo X Audiência

Segundos: 30, 28, 26, 24, 22, 20, 18, 16, 14, 12, 10, 8, 6, 4, 2, 0

0% 10% 20% 30% 40% 50% 60% 70% 80% 90% 100%

Audiência

Tempo para carregar o vídeo — Linear (Tempo para carregar o vídeo)

Source: Own figure

Chart Fact Sheet:
Features:

The longer the video takes to load, the smaller the increase in audience;
A user who wants to watch content waits for it to load and a user who is more sensitive and needs a shorter waiting time, i.e. satisfactory availability, also tends to watch the video in its entirety. Both of these characteristics work against each other.
A tendency towards stability, equality in the effects, because the two factors are joint and compensate for each other.

5.3.2.3 Verified Sample Statistics

With the analysis received by the data, it is necessary to know to what extent these conclusions can be classified as reliable to represent the whole. The literature tells us that the mathematical corollary showing the number of samples required for an acceptable level of assertiveness is expressed by Equation 6 below. The margin of error works as a probability density function, so we have the calculation for a sample (NSS, 2017; Pegg & Weisstein, 2017; Smith, 2013).

Number of Samples Required =

$$(\text{Z-score})^2 * \text{Desvio Padrão}*(1\text{-Desvio Padrão}) / (\text{Margem de Erro})^2 \quad (6)$$

The variable described as 'Z-score' denotes reliability, the maximum 'Standard Deviation' for very large or unknown populations should be set to 0.5 and the 'Margin of Error' is expressed as a percentage. It should be noted that these calculations are valid for a Gaussian distribution. This usually occurs for large populations of data, and this concept is related to the Law of Large Numbers. It is therefore confirmed that this is valid for an environment of the order of the data studied. That is, with around 2 quadrillion views a year and 1.3 billion users. Figure 61 shows what a Gaussian distribution, also known as a normal distribution, looks like. The image in Figure 61 shows that 68% of the population is within 1 standard deviation of the mean, plus or minus. 95% are within 2 standard deviations of the mean and 99.7% of the population are within 3 standard deviations (NSS, 2017; Pegg & Weisstein, 2017; Smith, 2013; Kernler, 2014).

Figure 61 Gaussian distribution.

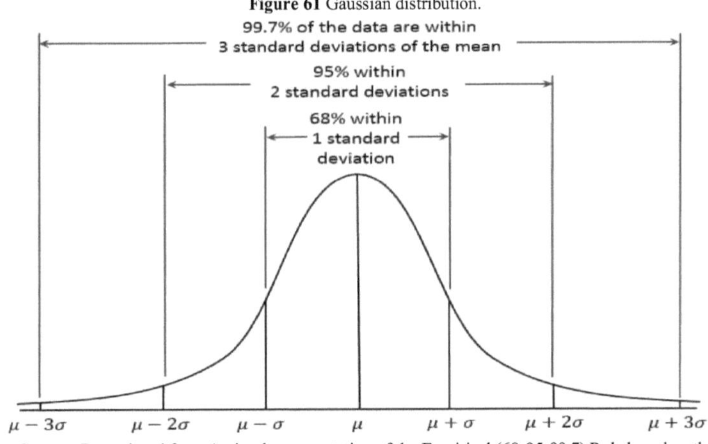

Source: Reproduced from A visual representation of the Empirical (68-95-99.7) Rule based on the normal distribution (Kernler, 2014).

For a reliability level of 99% with a 1% margin of error, 16,590 samples are needed, as seen in Equation (7). For a reliability level of 95% with a 5% margin of error, 385 samples are needed, as shown in Equation (8). And for 90% reliability with a 10% margin of error, 68 samples are needed, as shown by the calculations in Equation (9).

$$(((2.576)^2)* 0.5 * (1-0.5)) / (0.01)^2 = 16{,}589.44 \quad (7)$$

$$((1.96)^2)* 0.5 * (1-0.5)) / (0.05)^2 = 384.16 \quad (8)$$

$$((1.645)^2)* 0.5 * (1-0.5)) / (0.10)^2 = 67.65 \quad (9)$$

In view of the above, it is necessary to point out that such calculations apply to large quantities, from the order of millions to more, which are unknown and difficult to measure precisely and which tend to infinity. In addition, it is always expected that such quantities will follow a normal distribution, which should solidify as sampling increases (NSS, 2017; Pegg & Weisstein, 2017; Smith, 2013).

Continuing in this vein, it is necessary to quantify which level the 1281 samples fall into. Solving Equation (10) is therefore necessary in order to obtain these validation answers for this number of experiments. Looking at the equations previously solved and the number 1281, it is estimated that the reliability of 97% is adequate, so the Z-score for this level is 2.17009. This validates that the data captured in the experiments has a reliability of 97% with a margin of error of plus or minus 3.03% (NSS, 2017; Pegg & Weisstein, 2017; Smith, 2013).

$$((2.17009)^2) * (0.5) * (1-0.5) / ((x)^2) = 1281 \qquad (10)$$

$$x = 0.0303161$$

$$x = 3.03\%$$

CONCLUSION

The undeniable and growing importance of Internet protocol-based networks for transmitting audiovisual content requires more attention every day. And, since its inception, mechanisms for assigning controls have been an incessant and necessary quest. The aim of this work is to create mechanisms that bring assertiveness to this ecosystem that has taken on the role of traditional television broadcasting over the Internet. In this way, the methodologies proposed for assigning control mechanisms to the IP network environment proved to be capable of being implemented. The objectives set were achieved through mathematical comparisons and computationally implementable algorithms. And their products were designed to capture the desired information.

The first methodology, comprising the mathematical analysis of Broadcast TV and Stream IP throughput, demonstrated the importance of considering content delivery strategies for live and non-live broadcasts, based on the throughput cost of the channel when opting for one option or the other, or a mixture of both. Taking into account these calculations and the characteristics of the technologies, it is assessed that for live events for numerous content consumers, delivery via traditional television is currently proving impossible to replace, since the channel has a strong tendency not to support such demand if it is transferred to IP technology. In summary, the Technical-Mathematical Comparison demonstrates the cost in terms of throughput and the challenge in terms of design/infrastructure demand of making IP Streaming viable as a replacement for Broadcast TV, especially in the case of live transmissions, taking into account the definition of Digital TV.

In the second methodology, an algorithm was demonstrated with mechanisms to employ a network utility at the users' and/or devices' end, allowing them to gauge the availability of resources. Since the user pays for the Internet connection, to an ISP, and/or for the content they want to receive to a CDN, for example. And if we take into account that what most affects the availability of the network connection is video consumption. This software has proven to be a useful tool for continuously checking the availability of the connection with any resources that need to be checked. It brings assertiveness and a defense mechanism, i.e. measurement, to the user's end. This allows connection availability to be measured and charged to their respective providers using the data recorded from the tests carried out over a given period. In short, the Availability Measurement Software consolidates an efficient tool due to its low cost in terms of throughput and processing, and is effective in segregating, testing and charging all the parties involved in the content delivery chain: CDN, ISP, Provider, Equipment, Applications, etc.

For the third methodology, coding was programmed to measure the audience associated with the availability of videos from the largest provider of this type of content today. The aim was to observe the end user's point of view in order to achieve the objective, following the analogy used in the traditional TV broadcasting environment. With the differentiation provided by the different types of times duly categorized for this purpose of monitoring user interaction. To achieve this goal, the algorithm was computationally implemented in two parts: the client and the server, which aggregates all the data from all the tests of all the consumers who have the extension installed. The commercial and technical motivation for verifying the audience is the same as for traditional TV, given that on-demand IP content has taken over this role on a daily basis. The results obtained show that this is a tool that fulfills this functionality, making it possible to bring to the IP world an assertiveness that has so far only been present on TV, according to the literature. Therefore, it can be concluded that the Software for Audience Capture Associated with Video Stream Availability monitors the edge of the network, in a similar way to the TV meter, allowing this assertiveness to be brought to IP Video Delivery. It proved to be an efficient, effective and multifaceted tool, capturing relevant times to assess how Quality of Service affects Quality of Experience. The data allows for video-by-video, user-by-user, device-by-device analysis, centralizing everything in the cloud and at a low cost in terms of throughput and processing on both the client and the server.

By analyzing the data captured to measure availability and audience, the comparisons, calculations and plots make it possible to draw a number of relevant conclusions. These include the fact that the relationship between audience and availability is intrinsic, so that one feeds the other. It can also be seen that audience is negatively affected by unavailability. On the other hand, the Number of Subscribers and the Number of Views positively affect availability and audience above certain ranges. Also, the fact that unavailability is so frequent raises the question as to whether the low overall audience is due to the significant amount of negative interference inserted by the IP ecosystem. That is, whether it is due to the exhibition or the production, since it has been proven that there is a negative effect on packet network transmission. In addition, the use of Mobile Networks has low initial latency, but deteriorates over the course of the videos, with several pauses for loading and/or buffering. This makes the Quality of Experience variable, with low reliability. Continuing with this analysis, it can be concluded that connection masking highlights the lack of CDN infrastructure, even when using broadband. This proves that, even with a good connection, if the algorithms are prevented from working, the tendency is for them to deteriorate. In other words, the quality of IP video delivery depends directly on these algorithms present in the architecture of the audiovisual content delivery network. In this way, it is established that if privacy is desired when transmitting via IP Stream, the quality of the service and consequently of the experience is significantly impaired, even if the user's connection is at satisfactory levels. In addition, it is clear that the tests carried out are statistically valid, showing relevant indications and proving the efficiency and effectiveness of the tool and the analysis.

As you can see, the relationship between availability and audience is inherent, the parameters requested and the analyses chosen to be cataloged are satisfactory. It should also be emphasized that this issue is always affected by the location, device and network, or rather connection. In addition, it is emphasized that the transmissions that most affect video delivery are demonstrated when using mobile networks and when masking the connection in order to obtain privacy. After all, these two situations do not yet have an adaptable solution, as they prevent the algorithms that feed the CDNs from working properly, since we are continually changing routes in both cases, forcing a reorganization of the content delivery network. It can therefore be concluded that the road to IP networks is long and the challenge remains great despite considerable and constant developments, since this mode places the bottleneck in the physical environment, with a high price tag for building infrastructure. It is therefore proposed that an Alliance for the delivery of Hybrid Solutions has a greater chance of delivering quality audiovisuals, i.e. Broadcast and Broadband must coexist synergistically.

SUGGESTIONS FOR FUTURE WORK

As suggestions for possible future work, the steps implied below are intended as a way to inspire future studies that delve deeper into the issues addressed:

- The dissemination of the Extension in order to have a considerable sample of users and thus achieve a volume of data that allows the reading, abstraction of intelligence on the IP ecosystem in a consistent and continuous way;
- The release discusses the data captured from a large volume of users;
- The study of development feasibility to build a solution that is multisite, multi-browser and multi-device. It should certainly be based on a low-level language that can observe communication at all times.

REFERENCES

Alhir, 2003. Learning UML. Newton, Massachusetts, United States of America. Publisher: O'Reilly Media. 304p. ISBN: 0596003447, 978-0596003449.

Arthemia, 2017. Unified Modeling Language (UML) and Software Modeling Resources, News and Tools. Arthemia. Available at: < http://www.umlzone.com/>. Accessed on: February, 03, 2017.

Babatunde, O. and Al-Debagy, O.; 2014. A Comparative Review Of Internet Protocol Version 4 (IPv4) and Internet Protocol Version 6 (IPv6). International Journal of Computer Trends and Technology (IJCTT). Vol. 13, Number 1, p. 10-13, Jul 2014. ISSN: 2231-5381.
Available at: <http://arxiv.org/ftp/arxiv/papers/1407/1407.2717.pdf>. Accessed on: March, 25, 2016.

Baldini, G., Karanasios, S., Allen, D., Vergari, F.; 2014. Survey of Wireless Communication Technologies for Public Safety. IEEE COMMUNICATIONS SURVEYS & TUTORIALS. ISSN: 1553-877X. Vol. 16, No. 2, p. 619-641. DOI: 10.1109/SURV.2013.082713.00034 .

Bedicks Jr., G.; 2008. TUNER-DEMODULATOR FOR THE BRAZILIAN DIGITAL TV SYSTEM (in Portuguese). Doctoral Thesis. Electrical Engineering Faculty. University of Sao Paulo. Available at: <http://www.teses.usp.br/teses/disponiveis/3/3142/tde- 26092008-101922/en-br.php>. Accessed on: March, 25, 2016.

Buyya, R., Pathan, M., Vakali, A.; 2008. Content Delivery Networks. Berlin, Germany. Publisher: Springer. 417p. ISBN: 978-3-540-77886-8.

Chai, B.; 2014. 'True Detective' Finale Crashes HBO Go. Wall Street Journal. March 9. Available at: <http://blogs.wsj.com/speakeasy/ 2014/03/09/users-report-problems-on-hbo-go-as-true-detective-finale-airs/>. Accessed on: March 25, 2016.

Chaves de Oliveira *et al*, 2016, Chaves de Oliveira *et al*, 2016 B. Capturing Video Stream Audience Over IP Networks. SET INTERNATIONAL JOURNAL OF BROADCAST ENGINEERING, v. 2, p. 9-12, 2016; Medium: Digital. Homepage: ; Series: 2016; ISSN/ISBN: 24469246.

Christensson, P.; 2014. ISP Definition. Tech Terms Computer Dictionary. Available at: <http://www.techterms.com/definition/isp>. Accessed on: March, 25, 2016.

Cloonan, T. and Allen, J.; 2011. Competitive Analysis of Adaptive Video Streaming Implementations - White Paper. ARRIS. Available at: <http://www.arrisi .com/dig_lib/white_papers/_docs/Comp_Analysis_Adaptive_ Video.pd>. Accessed on: March, 25, 2016.

DARPA; 1981. RFC: 791 - INTERNET PROGRAM - PROTOCOL SPECIFICATION. Defense Advanced Research Projects Agency. Available at: <https://tools.ietf.org/html/rfc791>. Accessed on: March 25, 2016.

Deering, S. and Hinden, R.; 1998. RFC: 2460 - Internet Protocol, Version 6 (IPv6) Specification. Defense Advanced Research Projects Agency. Available at: <https://tools.ietf.org/html/rfc2460>. Accessed on: March 25, 2016.

DICIO; 2016. Audience - Meaning of Audience. Dicio: Online Portuguese Dictionary, definitions and meanings of over 400,000 words. All words from A to Z. Available at: <http://www.dicio.com.br/audiencia/>. Accessed on: March, 25, 2016.

Doeven, J.; 2013. TRENDS IN BROADCASTING: AN OVERVIEW OF DEVELOPMENTS. ITU - International Telecommunication Union. Telecommunication Development Bureau. Available at: <http://www.itu.int/en/ITU-D/Technology/Documents/Broadcasting/TrendsinBroadcasting.pdf>. Accessed on: March 25, 2016.

Dresch *et al*, 2015. Design Science Research: A Method for Science and Technology Advancement 2015th Edition. Berlin, Germany. Publisher: Springer. 161p. ISBN:

9783319073736.
Edwards, J.; 2013. TV Is Dying, And Here Are The Stats That Prove It. Business Insider Inc. Available at: <http://www.businessinsider.com/cord-cutters-and-the-death-of-tv- 2013-11>. Accessed on: March, 25, 2016.
Ellacott, J.; 2014. Video Streaming Driving Impressive Growth in Video Content Delivery Market: TechNavio Trends. TECHNAVIO. Infiniti Research Limited. Available at: <http://www.technavio.com/blog/video-streaming-driving-impressivegrowth-in-video- content-delivery-market-technavio-trends>. Accessed on: March 25, 2016.
Frost, V.; 2014. The TV is dead, long live television. The Guardian. December 9. Available at:<http://www.theguardian.com/commentisfree/2014/dec/09/tv-dead-long-live-
television-format-consuming>. Accessed on: March, 25, 2016.
Greenfield, R.; 2012. NBC Claims Super Bowl Streaming Victory, But Viewers Cry 'Fail'.
The Wire.The Atlantic Monthly Group. Available at: <http://www.thewire.com/technology/2012/02/nbc-claims-super-bowl-streaming-victory- viewers-cry-fail/48409/>. Accessed on: March 25, 2016.
Hughes, A. M.; 2010. Phone and Broadband as Commodities. Database Marketing Institute - Telecom Articles. Available at: <http://www.dbmarketing.com/2010/03/phone-and- broadband-as-commodities/>. Accessed on: March 25, 2016.
ITU; 2003. The Birth of Broadband - Media Fact Sheet . International Telecommunication
Union (ITU). Available at: <http://www.itu.int/osg/spu /publications/birthofbroadband/faq.html>. Accessed on: March, 25, 2016.
Kaduoka *et al*, 2016. STREAMING AND DISTRIBUTION IP: CHALLENGES. SET EXPO PROCEEDINGS, v. 2, p. 180-183, 2016; Media: Digital. Homepage: ; Series: 2016; ISSN/ISBN: 24470481.
Katel, P.; 2014. Future of TV Can traditional television thrive in the Internet Age? CQ RESEARCHER. April 11. Vol. 24, Issue 14, p. 314-336.
Kenyon, C. and Cheliotis, G.; 2001. Stochastic models for telecom commodity prices. Computer Networks. Elsevier. Vol. 6, p. 533-555. ISSN: 1389-1286. Dispornvel em: <http://citeseerx.ist.psu.edu/viewdoc/download;jsessionid=A814324BD7305852C2E72708 960A263B?doi=10.1.1.83.7669&rep=rep1&type=pdf>. Accessed on: March, 25, 2016.
Kernler, 2014. A visual representation of the Empirical (68-95-99.7) Rule based on the normal distribution. Wikipedia. Available at: <https://en.wikipedia.org/wiki/File: Empirical_ Rule.PNG>. Accessed August 30, 2017.
Khanafer, M., Guennoun, M., Mouftah, H.; 2014. A Survey of Beacon-Enabled IEEE 802.15.4 MAC Protocols in Wireless Sensor Networks. IEEE COMMUNICATIONS SURVEYS & TUTORIALS. ISSN: 1553-877X. Vol. 16, No. 2, p. 856-876. DOI: 10.1109/SURV.2013.112613.00094 .
Krishnan & Sitaraman; 2013. Video Stream Quality Impacts Viewer Behavior: Inferring Causality Using Quasi-Experimental Designs. IEEE/ACM Transactions on Networking. Volume: 21, Issue: 6 Pages: 2001 - 2014, DOI: 10.1109/TNET.2013.2281542.
Lewin, 2014. For the Love of Physics (Walter Lewin's Last Lecture). For the Allure of Physics. YouTube. Available at: <https://www.youtube.com/watch?v= 4a0FbQdH3dY&t=1976s>. Accessed on: August, 30, 2017.
McMillan, G.; 2013. Viewers Are Flocking to Streaming Video Content - And So Are Advertisers. WIRED. Available at: <http://www.wired.com /2013/03/streaming-video-advertising/>. Accessed on: March, 25, 2016.

Microsoft; 2015. Microsoft TechNet - PING. Microsoft Inc. Available at: <http://technet.microsoft.com/en-us/library/bb490968.aspx>. Accessed on: March, 25, 2016.
Mozilla; 2015. Mozilla Firefox. Mozilla. Available at: <http://www.mozilla.org/en-US/firefox/new/>. Accessed on: Margo, 25, 2016.
N-TRON, 2014. White paper: Network Availability. N-TRON Corporation: THE INDUSTRIAL NETWORK COMPANY Available at: <http://www.n-tron.com/tech_docs.php>. Accessed on: Margo, 25, 2016.
Nunes, R.; 2011. Web portal for continuous Internet access Quality of Service measurement. Masters dissertation. Technical Superior Institute. Technical University of Lisbon.
NSS; 2017. Sample Size Calculator. National Statistical Service - Australian Bureau of Statistics. Available at: <http://www.nss.gov.au/nss/home.nsf/pages/Sample+size+calcul ator>. Accessed on: June, 10, 2017.
Oberortner, E., Sobernig, S., Zdun, U., Dustdar, S.; 2012. Monitoring Performance-Related QoS Properties in Service-Oriented Systems: A Pattern-Based Architectural Decision Model. Publication Repository of the Computer Science Faculty. University of Vienna. Available at: <http://eprints.cs.univie.ac.at/3017/1/sequence-oberortner.pdf>. Accessed on: March, 25, 2016.
Object Management Group (OMG), 2017. Unified Modeling Language. Object Management Group, Inc. Available at: <http://www.uml.org//>. Accessed on: February, 03, 2017.
Octoshape & T-Mobile; 2014. Transitioning from Broadcast TV to Broadband TV with LiveStream Perform - White Paper. Octoshape Inc and T-Mobile Inc. Available at: <http://www.octoshape.com/terms-of-use/whitepapers/transitioning-from-broadcast-tv-to- broadband-tv-with-livestream-perform/>. Accessed on: Margo, 25, 2016.
Ofcom; 2014. Infrastructure Report 2014. Ofcom. Independent regulator and competition authority for the UK communications industries. Available at: <http://stakeholders.ofcom.org.uk/binaries/research/infrastructure/2014/infrastructure-14.pdf>. Accessed on: Margo, 25, 2016.
Oliveira, V. C., Bedicks Jr., G. and Akamine, C.; 2015 A. METHODOLOGY TO ASSES IP CONNECTION AVAILABILITY: A PREREQUISITE FOR FEASIBLE VIDEO STREAM THROUGH CDNs. Journal of Computer Science. ISSN: 1549-3636. Vol. 11, Issue 2, p. 426-437. DOI: 10.3844/jcssp.2015.426.437.
Oliveira, V. C., Bedicks Jr., G. and Akamine, C.; 2015 B. IP VIDEO DELIVERY COST: AN ANALYSIS ON CHANNEL AVAILABILITY FOR LIVE AND NON-LIVE STREAM EVENTS. In: 2015 - 64th - IEEE Broadcast Symposium, 2015, Orlando, FL, USA. 2015 - 64th - IEEE Broadcast Symposium Technical Program. New York, NY, USA: IEEE Institute of Electrical and Electronics Engineers / IEEE Broadcast Technology Society, IEEE BTS, 2015. v. 64.
Oliveira, V., Mota, A., Mota, L.; 2013 A. IMPACTS OF APPLICATION USAGE AND LOCAL HARDWARE ON THE THROUGHPUT OF COMPUTER NETWORKS WITH DESKTOP VIRTUALIZATION. American Journal of Applied Sciences. ISSN: 1546-9239. Vol. 10, Issue 1, p. 117-122. DOI: 10.3844/ajassp.2013.117.122 .
Oliveira, V, Yano, I., Mota, A., Mota, L.; 2013 B. FEASIBILITY OF DESKTOP VIRTUALIZATION PER SOFTWARE SERVICES AND LOCAL HARDWARE BASED ON THE NETWORK THROUGHPUT. Journal of Computer Science. ISSN: 1549-3636.
Vol. 9, Issue 7, p. 827-837. DOI: 10.3844/jcssp.2013.827.837 .
Oliveira, V.; 2012. Impacts of the variation of applications and of local hardware on the

flow rate of computer networks with desktop virtualization (in portuguese). Masters dissertation. Electrical Engineering Faculty. Pontifical Catholic University of Campinas.
Oracle Corporation; 2015. MySQL -The world's most popular open source database. ORACLE. Available at: <http://www.mysql.com/>. Accessed on: March, 25, 2016.
Pivotal Software; 2015. Spring Tool Suite. SPRING. Available at: <http://spring.io/>. Accessed on: March, 25, 2016.
Pegg & Weisstein; 2017. "Margin of Error." From MathWorld--A Wolfram Web Resource. Wolfram Research, Inc. Available at: <http://mathworld.wolfram.com/MarginofError. html>. Accessed on: June, 10, 2017.
Ross and Kurose; 2013. Computer Networking: A Top-Down Approach 6th Edition. London, United Kingdom. Publisher: Pearson . 864p. ISBN-13: 9780132856201.
Rouse, M.; 2011. Definition: Content Delivery Network (CDN). TechTarget. Search AWS. Available at: <http://searchaws.techtarget.com /definition/content-delivery-network- CDN>. Accessed on: March, 25, 2016.
Shannon, C.; 1948. A Mathematical Theory of Communication. The Bell System Technical Journal. Vol. 27, p. 379-423, 623-656.
Sharma, A. and FitzGerald, D.; 2014. ABC's Oscars Streaming Outage Shows Web Limitations for TV Networks - Traffic Overload During Academy Awards Tested Live-Streaming Capabilities. Wall Street Journal. March 3. Disponível em: <http://online.wsj.com/news/articles/SB100014240527023045850045794172306390018 94>. Accessed on: March 25, 2016.
Simon; 1996. The Sciences of the Artificial - 3rd Edition. Cambridge, Massachusetts, USA. Publisher: MIT Press. 215p. ISBN: 978-0262691918.
Smith; 2013. Determining Sample Size: How to Ensure You Get the Correct Sample Size. Qualtrics. Available at <https://www.qualtrics.com/blog/determining-sample-size/>. Accessed on: June, 10, 2017.
Statista; 2015 A. Statista Inc. Statistics and facts about YouTube. Available at: <http://www.statista.com/topics/2019/youtube/>. Accessed on: April, 16, 2016.
Statista; 2015 B. Statista Inc. Global market share held by the leading internet browsers from January 2012 to December 2015. Available at: <http://www.statista.com/statistics/268254/market-share-of-internet-browsers-worldwide- since-2009/>. Accessed on: April, 16, 2016.
Statista; 2016. Statista Inc. YouTube - Statista Dossier. Available at: <http://www.statista.com/topics/2019/youtube/>. Accessed on: April, 16, 2016.
Statistic Brain; 2016. Statistic Brain Research Institute. YouTube Company Statistics. Available at: <http://www.statisticbrain.com/youtube-statistics/>. Accessed on: June, 11, 2016.
STOLFI, G.; 2008. Temporal Interleaving Through Fourier transform - A ROBUST METHOD FOR TRANSMISSION OF DIGITAL TV SIGNALS.
DOCTORAL THESIS. Electrical Engineering Faculty. University of Sao Paulo.
Tanenbaum & Wetherall; 2010. Computer Networks 5th Edition. New Jersey, United States of America. Publisher: Prentice Hall. 960p. ISBN: 0132126958, 978-0132126953.
TECHNAVIO; 2014. Global Video CDN Market 2014-2018. TECHNAVIO. Infiniti Research Limited. March 28. 98p. SKU: IRTNTR3432.
Tomcat; 2015. Apache Tomcat. Apache Software Foundation. Available at: <http://tomcat.apache.org/>. Accessed on: March, 25, 2016.
Trend Micro; 2015. BYOD - Consumerization of IT & Mobility - Trend Micro UK. Trend Micro (EMEA) Limited. Available at: <http://www.trendmicro.ae/ enterprise/consumerization/>. Accessed on: March 25, 2016.
Vanover, R.; 2008. IPv6 and IPv4 mixed mode nodes inevitable. CBS Interactive - TechRepublic. Available at: <http://www.techrepublic.com /blog/data-center/ipv6-and-

ipv4-mixed-mode-nodes-inevitable/>. Accessed on: March, 25, 2016.
YouTube; 2017. YouTube Press Statistics. YouTube. Dispornvelem :
<https://www.youtube.com/yt/press/statistics.html>. Accessed on: June, 11, 2016.

I want morebooks!

Buy your books fast and straightforward online - at one of world's fastest growing online book stores! Environmentally sound due to Print-on-Demand technologies.

Buy your books online at
www.morebooks.shop

Kaufen Sie Ihre Bücher schnell und unkompliziert online – auf einer der am schnellsten wachsenden Buchhandelsplattformen weltweit! Dank Print-On-Demand umwelt- und ressourcenschonend produzi ert.

Bücher schneller online kaufen
www.morebooks.shop

Printed by Books on Demand GmbH, Norderstedt / Germany